Coping with Depression in Young People

A Guide for Parents

Because your family matters . . .

The Wiley *Family Matters* series highlights topics that are important to the everyday lives of family members. Each book tackles a common problem or difficult situation, such as teenage troubles, new babies or problems in relationships, and provides easily understood advice from authoritative professionals. The *Family Matters* series is designed to provide expert advice to ordinary people struggling with everyday problems and bridges the gap between the professional and client. Each book also offers invaluable help to practitioners as extensions to the advice they can give in sessions, and helps trainees to understand the issues clients face.

Titles in the series:

Coping with Depression in Young People

A Guide for Parents

Carol Fitzpatrick

Professor of Child Psychiatry

John Sharry

Principal Social Worker

JOHN WILEY & SONS, LTD

Other Wiley Editorial Offices

John Wiley & Sons Inc., 111 River Street, Hoboken, NJ 07030, USA

Jossey-Bass, 989 Market Street, San Francisco, CA 94103-1741, USA

Wiley-VCH Verlag GmbH, Boschstr. 12, D-69469 Weinheim, Germany

John Wiley & Sons Australia Ltd, 33 Park Road, Milton, Queensland 4064, Australia

John Wiley & Sons (Asia) Pte Ltd, 2 Clementi Loop #02-01, Jin Xing Distripark, Singapore 129809

John Wiley & Sons Canada Ltd, 22 Worcester Road, Etobicoke, Ontario, Canada M9W 1L1

Wiley also publishes its books in a variety of electronic formats. Some content that appears in print may
not be available in electronic books.

Library of Congress Cataloging-in-Publication Data
Fitzpatrick, Carol.
 Coping with depression in young people : a guide for parents / Carol
Fitzpatrick, John Sharry.
  p. cm. – (Family matters)
 Includes bibliographical references and index.
 ISBN 0-470-85755-2 (Paper : alk. paper)
 1. Depression in adolescence – Popular works. 2. Depression in
adolescence – Treatment – Popular works. 3. Teenagers – Mental
health – Popular works. I. Sharry, John. II. Title.
 III. Family matters (John Wiley & Sons)
 RJ506.D4F55 2004
 616.85'27'00835 – dc22   2003019767

British Library Cataloguing in Publication Data
A catalogue record for this book is available from the British Library

ISBN 0-470-85755-2

Project management by Originator, Gt Yarmouth, Norfolk (typeset in 11½/13pt Imprint)
Printed and bound in Great Britain by TJ International Ltd, Padstow, Cornwall
This book is printed on acid-free paper responsibly manufactured from sustainable forestry in which at
least two trees are planted for each one used for paper production.

Contents

About the authors

Professor Carol Fitzpatrick is Professor of Child Psychiatry at University College Dublin and a Consultant Child and Adolescent Psychiatrist at the Mater Hospital and The Children's Hospital, Temple Street, in Dublin. She is author of many research papers about mental health in young people and has a particular interest in depression and self-harm in young people.

Dr John Sharry is Principal Social Worker at the Mater Hospital and is a Director of The Brief Therapy Group in Dublin. He is the author of four self-help books for parents, including *Parent Power: Bringing up Responsible Children and Teenagers* (John Wiley & Sons, 2003) and *When Parents Separate: Helping Children Cope* (Veritas, 2001). He is also the author of three psychotherapy books: *Solution-focused Groupwork* (Sage, 2001), *Becoming a Solution Detective: A strengths-based Guide to Brief Therapy* (BT Press, 2001) and the forthcoming *Counselling Children, Adolescents and Families* (Sage, 2004).

Both authors are experienced clinicians who have worked with many young people and their families coping with depression. They are joint authors of The Parents Plus Programmes, video-based courses for parents coping with a variety of emotional and behavioural difficulties in their children and teenagers, which are widely used in the UK and Ireland. See www.parentsplus.ie

Preface

Being a parent is one of the most difficult but rewarding jobs around. As parents, we want to get it right, yet no training is provided and we mostly muddle along, hoping that things will work out. As parents, we are reassured that things are going OK if our children are well, seem reasonably happy at school, have some friends and some interests in life, and we can communicate with them at some level. Parents of teenagers expect the mood changes, the highs and lows, the rows and challenges to authority that are part of normal adolescence. But being the parent of a depressed young person can be a very daunting, overwhelming experience. Depression is a common problem in young people, affecting about 5% of teenagers and 2% of younger children. It often produces dramatic and frightening changes in young people's behaviour, emotional responses and relationships with those closest to them.

Discovering that your child has depression is usually a very difficult period for parents. You may have been aware for some time that something was wrong, yet have found it hard to know what. You may be unsure how to respond to your child and fear making a bad situation worse. You know your child so well, yet may barely recognise the person your child seems to have become. You may not know what help is available, or even whether or not you should seek help. Your deepest fears of lifetime mental illness or suicide may be unspoken. You wonder has any other parent felt as helpless as you.

This book is written in response to parents' requests for recommended reading material to help them understand their young person who is depressed, to show them what they can do to help, to give them realistic hope that things will improve and to enable them and all the family survive and come through what can be a very challenging situation.

Acknowledgements

We would like to thank all our professional colleagues, family and friends for their support in writing this book. Their support and encouragement made the journey much easier. We would also like to acknowledge all the young people and parents whom we have had the privilege of working with over the years and whose stories constitute this book. We have been deeply impressed and moved by their never-ending resourcefulness in the face of adversity. Their courage continues to inspire us.

What is depression?

Depression is an emotion we are all familiar with. A bleakness of thought, a feeling of irritation toward those closest to us, a sense of emptiness, a question about what life is for, an inability to feel joy or pleasure – most of us have gone through times in our lives when we have had some or all of these feelings. Mostly they occur when we are tired or overburdened, when we have had a row with someone close to us or when an important relationship is not going smoothly. We usually can explain to ourselves why we feel the way we do and can reassure ourselves that these feelings will pass. This is depression, *the feeling*, part of the vast range of normal emotion that makes us human and that is as much a part of our ordinary experience as is joy, anger, fear or happiness.

When we hear somebody described as being depressed, we imagine that we have an idea of how they are feeling, based on our own experiences. We expect that their feelings of depression are a reaction to something negative that is happening in their lives, and we expect them to try to get over their depression – 'to snap out of it'. This is what most people understand when they hear the term 'depression' being used.

When mental health professionals use the term 'depression', they usually mean a *depressive disorder*, something that has some shared features with what is described above, but something that also has important differences. The term 'depressive disorder' implies that the person has a number of symptoms, including depressed mood, as described above, only usually to a much more profound degree, *and* they have what is called 'functional impairment' – in other words, they are handicapped in their ability to get on with life, to carry out their everyday life's activities. The classification systems used by mental health professionals in diagnosing depressive disorders are shown in Tables 1.1 and 1.2.

Many of the symptoms shown in Tables 1.1 and 1.2 are common in young people and probably in most of us from time to time, and do not mean we are suffering from a depressive disorder. What is important is the combination and severity of the symptoms and their effect on everyday life and the ability to function. In young people, irritability is often particularly marked, leading the young person to be in conflict with family, friends and teachers. This can lead to a vicious cycle of depression → conflict → further depression.

When depressed young people and those around them get into a vicious cycle like this, things can seem completely stuck. As a parent, you want to help your child, but you may feel angry and beaten back by his hostility or seeming indifference. It can feel as if there is no way forward. But there are ways of helping which can gradually 'unstick' situations like this, and these are dealt with in detail in the chapters ahead.

Classification systems for depressive disorders used by psychiatrists

Diagnosis of major depressive episode

Table 1.1. World Health Organization System (ICD-10*)

The individual usually suffers from depressed mood, loss of interest and enjoyment, and reduced energy leading to increased fatiguability and diminished activity. Marked tiredness after only slight effort is common. Other common symptoms are:

a   reduced concentration and attention;
b   reduced self-esteem and self-confidence;
c   ideas of guilt and unworthiness;
d   bleak and pessimistic views of the future;
e   ideas or acts of self-harm or suicide;
f   disturbed sleep;
g   diminished appetite.

The clinical presentation shows marked individual variations, and atypical presentations are particularly common in adolescence. In some cases anxiety, distress and motor agitation may be more prominent at times than the depression, and the mood change may also be masked by added features, such as irritability, excessive consumption of alcohol, histrionic behaviour and exacerbation of pre-existing phobic or obsessional symptoms, or by hypochondriacal preoccupations.

A duration of at least 2 weeks is usually required for diagnosis and episodes may be mild, moderate or severe.

* *The ICD-10 Classification of Mental and Behavioural Disorders: Clinical Descriptions and Diagnostic Guidelines*, World Health Organization, Geneva, 1992. Reproduced with permission. ICD-10 = International Classification of Diseases – 10th Revision.

Table 1.2. American System (DSM-IV*)

Five (or more) of the following symptoms have been present during the same 2-week period and represent a change from previous functioning; at least one of the symptoms is either (i) depressed mood or (ii) loss of interest or pleasure:

i   Depressed mood most of the day, nearly every day, as indicated by either subjective report (e.g., feels sad or empty) or observation made by others (e.g., appears tearful). Note: In children and adolescents, can be irritable mood.

ii Markedly diminished interest or pleasure in all, or almost all, activities most of the day, nearly every day (as indicated by either subjective account or observation made by others).

iii Significant weight loss when not dieting, or weight gain, or decrease or increase in appetite nearly every day. Note: In children consider failure to make expected weight gains.

iv Insomnia or hypersomnia nearly every day.

v   Psychomotor retardation or agitation nearly every day.

vi Fatigue or loss of energy nearly every day.

vii Feelings of worthlessness or excessive or inappropriate guilt.

viii Diminished ability to think or concentrate, or indecisiveness.

ix Recurrent thoughts of death, recurrent suicidal ideation without a specific plan, or a suicide attempt or a specific plan for committing suicide.

The symptoms must not be due to another mental illness, or to the effects of drugs or medical illness. They must cause significant distress or impairment in social, occupational or other important areas of functioning to warrant a diagnosis of Major Depressive Episode.

* *Diagnostic and Statistical Manual of Mental Disorders* (4th edn), American Psychiatric Association, Washington, DC, 1994. Reprinted with permission.

Depressive disorders come in all grades of severity from mild disorders where the person may have the symptoms listed and be less efficient, less affectionate, less spontaneous than they usually are, to very severe disorders where the person may be unable to get out of bed, unable to communicate, unable to eat or drink, all of which may become a medical emergency. There are all sorts of grades between these two extremes. While there is no such thing as a typical case of depressive disorder in a young person, each case being somewhat different just as no two people are the same, the following case history is a good example of a young teenager with a depressive disorder.

Case history

Sarah, aged 13, has not been to school for 8 weeks. She got the flu 3 months ago and was out of school for a fortnight. She was determined to get back as quickly as possible as she is a conscientious student who works very hard and who likes to be and expects to be at the top of her class. When she tried to go back she felt a sense of dread that is hard to describe. She gets this feeling whenever she is not at home, but it is most marked when she tries to go to school. She worries a great deal about missing school and falling behind her classmates. She has no special friend in her class but there were some girls she was quite friendly with who used to call to see how she was getting on when she was first sick, but they have stopped calling now. Sarah has little energy and sleeps more than usual. She would sleep longer but her mother wakes her each morning at her usual time

*for getting up for school in the hope that this will be
the day she will go, but she does not. Sarah is irritable and angry most of the time but especially so in
the mornings, and the atmosphere at home is very
strained.*

*Sarah's parents are at their wits' end. They took
Sarah to their general practitioner who gave her a
thorough check-up but could find nothing wrong.
Sarah's older brother thinks she is 'putting it on'
and nags his parents to 'get tough' with her. Her
father wonders if perhaps this might be the right
approach but holds back when he sees how unwell
she looks at times. Her mother alternates between
feeling sorry for Sarah and being very annoyed
with her as she is demanding and ungrateful – most
unlike 'the old Sarah'. Sarah's mother has herself
suffered from depression in the past and wonders if
this could be depression, but she feels overwhelmed by
the situation and is unsure where to turn.*

Depression in children and adolescents usually has some
of the above features but they may not always appear in
the classical way described above. The reasons for this are
many. Young people, particularly children, often do not
have the language to describe how they are feeling. They
experience the feelings, but are unable to describe them to
others. Older children and adolescents may have the
language, but are reluctant to talk about how they are
feeling, often believing that others may think they are
going mad, a fear they often have themselves. There
are no words that can adequately describe some of the
feelings experienced by some young people going
through a depressive disorder, and it is only when they

have recovered that they can describe what they have felt. The next section, 'What depression feels like', gives real life examples of descriptions by young people of how they felt when they were going through a depressive disorder. These examples are shown with the permission of the young people involved.

What depression feels like

Quotes from young people (see also Chapter 10 for further information and quotes on the experiences of young people):

It was like a dread inside, there all the time. When I was with my friends it would go away a bit, but it always came back.

Jack, aged 15

I started worrying about everything, even things that never bothered me before. I was so worried about being asked a question in school that I used to feel sick in the mornings. Some days I just could not go to school.

Nessa, aged 13

I was angry with everyone, they all annoyed me, particularly my mum who kept asking me what was wrong.

Laura, aged 14

I couldn't face anyone, I don't know why. I wanted to be dead, it was in my mind all the time, I couldn't stop thinking about my death and being dead. At least then I would stop feeling like this.

Sue, aged 15

Sometimes there'd be this feeling of being trapped, or perhaps overwhelmed. Other times there'd be a feeling of just being completely lost and not knowing what to do, and then the most frequent was probably one of complete and utter apathy for life, the universe and everything.

David, aged 16

I got very fatigued. I'd stay in bed for ever really. I just felt absolutely lousy and I got awful stomach pains as well, and awful headaches. So that's how I felt.

John, aged 15

How common is depression in young people?

Many research studies have been done which involve interviewing large numbers of ordinary young people and usually their parents as well. The interviews used are in-depth psychiatric interviews that allow a formal psychiatric diagnosis to be made. Studies of this type are fairly consistent in showing that about 5% of adolescents have a depressive disorder. This represents about 25 pupils in a secondary school with 500 pupils. Depression occurs in about 2% of older children and probably occurs in younger children, but accurate figures are not available for this age group. Depression occurs in children from all social backgrounds and is often associated with other emotional and behavioural problems. In childhood, depression seems to occur with equal frequency in boys and girls, but in adolescence it may be more common in girls. We are not sure about this, as adolescent boys are notoriously reticent about discussing their feelings with others and that includes the professionals who carry out research studies. It may be that adolescent boys are just as likely as girls to suffer from depression, but they show it in a different way (e.g., with more anger and impulsive hostility).

In childhood and adolescence, depression is usually unrecognised and untreated. The young person is often regarded as being moody, difficult, troubled or troublesome, but is rarely regarded as being depressed. This is partly because adults find it hard to imagine that children and adolescents could suffer from depression in much the same way as adults do, and partly because young people often express their pain in different ways to adults. Young people rarely complain of feeling depressed; they are more likely to complain of being fed up, bored or lonely. Or they may not complain at all, but instead act out their negative feelings, becoming hostile and aggressive to those who are often trying hardest to help them.

Tom's story

Tom, aged 14, seems to have had 'a total change of personality'. At least that is how his mother sees it. He has become moody, irritable and verbally abusive to the rest of the family and refuses to discuss what is wrong. He spends most of the time in his bedroom, taking his meals there and often locking himself in for hours on end. He no longer goes out and seems to have no interest in anything other than eating, which occupies a good deal of his time. He has put on a lot of weight which his mother attributes to his lack of activity and his overeating. She worries that he might be on drugs, but cannot think how he could get them as he rarely leaves the house and has no friends. He can be heard up at night when the rest of the family have gone to bed, but is unrousable in the mornings and would sleep until late afternoon if allowed to. Sometimes his mother allows this, as once he is awake the atmosphere in the house is almost unbearable. Occasionally, he has 'good days' when it is possible to talk to him, but he is most reluctant to talk, and tells his mother to 'get off my case'.

She knows about adolescent mood swings, having reared two other teenagers, and she wonders if this is an extreme case of normal adolescent behaviour.

(continued on p. 54)

Causes of depression

There have been huge advances in research into the causes of depressive disorders in recent times, but we are still some way from having a clear understanding. There is no single cause for depression, but we know that in many situations there is an interaction between a genetic vulnerability and adverse life events. Many young people have a history in their families of depressive disorders in their parents, aunts, uncles or grandparents. A family history of depression does not necessarily imply a genetic basis. A child who has grown up with a depressed family member may respond to adversity by behaving as they have seen others around them behave and, thus, they are more prone to develop depression as a kind of 'learned behaviour'. However, research has shown that genetic factors play an important role in many types of depression. What seems to be inherited is not a single gene for depression but rather a genetic vulnerability. It is likely that many people carry this vulnerability, but they may never experience significant depression. This may be because they never have a combination of things going wrong for them at a particular time, or because they have, in addition to their genetic vulnerability, one or many protective factors. Protective factors in children include a stable relationship with at least one parent and a positive, confident temperament.

Adverse life events that may predispose young people to develop depression include losses of various kinds, such as loss of a parent through separation or divorce, loss of self-esteem through bullying, abuse or failure. Living in situations of family conflict or where a parent is him or herself struggling with a mental health problem, such as alcoholism or depression, may also predispose a young person to develop depression. Most young people with chronic physical problems, such as cystic fibrosis, chronic renal failure or diabetes, do not develop depression, but some do, particularly in adolescence when for the first time they fully appreciate the nature of their physical problems. Some acute illnesses, such as glandular fever, may precipitate depression in young people, as may some other viral illnesses.

Very conscientious, perfectionistic young people seem to be more prone to develop depression than their more easy-going peers, but depression can occur in young people with any type of personality. There is only very rarely a single cause that can be identified. More commonly, there are a number of adverse factors, some of which may seem trivial to an outsider, that predispose a vulnerable young person to develop depression.

Young people with long-standing behaviour problems, learning difficulties or attention deficit hyperactivity disorder (ADHD) are more prone than usual to depression, probably due in part to the many negative experiences such children have had. These experiences include difficulties with friendships, academic failure and constant criticism. The self-esteem of such children tends to be very low, often hidden under an aggressive, brash exterior. In Chapter 3 we consider these special difficulties in more detail.

Is depression in young people more common now than in the past?

That is a difficult question to answer because we do not know how common depression was in the past. It is only within the past 15 to 20 years that accurate estimates are available about rates of depression in young people. The number of young people being referred to services for treatment of depression seems to be increasing, but that could be due to many factors, including more services being available and families being more willing to seek help.

What happens to young people with depression?

The outlook is good for most young people with depression. The depression tends to lift, whether or not they receive treatment. A recent study of a group of teenagers with depression showed that the depression was no longer present 2 years after the initial diagnosis in 80% of the group. Many young people with depressive disorders do not suffer from depression again, but in others there is a tendency for it to recur, particularly at times of stress or change in their lives, such as when they leave home, have a baby, lose a job or experience a broken relationship. This is by no means inevitable, but it does mean that part of the treatment of depression involves helping the young person and their family to be aware of the early symptoms of depression so that, should it recur, they can take active steps early on to prevent it developing into full-blown depression.

In rare cases the depression recurs at regular intervals or alternates with periods of elevated mood, which is called bipolar or manic depressive disorder. This type of disorder can be greatly helped or even prevented from recurring by particular treatment approaches that are outlined in Chapter 4.

Suicide is the greatest fear of all parents of depressed young people. This is entirely understandable given the stark rise in suicide rates in young people, especially young men, in recent times. But remember, depression is very common while suicide is still rare. It is probably not possible to prevent anyone of any age from killing themselves if they are truly determined to do so, but there are ways of reducing the risk. As a parent there is a lot you can do to deal with the fear of suicide and this is dealt with in Chapter 8.

While most young people with depression recover, it can take a long time. Two years out of the life of a teenager, when so much could be happening for them in terms of friendships, schoolwork, sport and fun, is too long. In many situations, you as a parent can help greatly. You probably cannot make the depression go away, but you can take active steps to ensure that your son/daughter gets all the help they need and that you and the family are there to support them, while getting on with your own life in a way that gives a message of hope to your teenager.

How to recognise depression in young people

It can be difficult to recognise depression in young people. Many teenagers have 'ups and downs' in their mood, being outgoing, pleasant, happy and confident one day and withdrawn, silent and brooding the next. There is no sharp dividing line between these 'normal mood swings' of adolescence and depressive disorders, but there are some pointers to help parents decide if their young person is depressed.

Which young people are most likely to get depressed?

Depression can affect anyone, but some young people are more at risk than others. These include: those who have had previous emotional or behavioural problems; those with attention deficit hyperactivity disorder (ADHD);

those who have suffered physical, emotional or sexual abuse; those who have difficulties fitting in because of problems with social relationships, in particular those who find it hard to get along with peers. (In Chapter 3, we explore further how depression affects children with special needs and other difficulties.) The teenage years may be particularly problematic for these young people, because it is the time in life when there is enormous pressure to conform, to be the same as your peers.

Young people with a history of depression in a close relative are also at increased risk of depression. If you have suffered from depression yourself in the past, you may be very alert to the possibility of depression in your teenager.

Parents and teachers are the key people to recognise the signs of depression in young people. They know them better than mental health professionals and are in the best position to recognise changes in mood or behaviour that may indicate a depressive disorder. Young people themselves rarely complain of being depressed. They may say they are 'bored' or 'tired' or 'fed up', but it is distinctly unusual for a depressed young person to recognise depression in themselves, or to seek help. They are dependent on those around them to see beyond their difficult, offputting behaviour, and to seek help on their behalf.

Changes in mood and behaviour

While short-lived mood changes occur in most adolescents, changes in mood and behaviour that don't go away and that cause suffering to the young person and prevent his or her getting on with life may signal a depressive disorder.

Case history

John, aged 14, has always been a shy, sensitive person. As a child he was happy in the company of his family who enjoyed his dry sense of humour and his unusual interests – he enjoyed collecting matchbox labels from around the world and spent long periods cataloguing his collection. Primary school was a mixed experience for John – he got on well with some teachers and not with others, and had no close friends although some children did enjoy his company.

Things started to change when John moved to secondary school at 13 years of age. Although he knew many of the other pupils who were starting with him, as they had been in his class in primary school, they seemed to form friendships more quickly than he did and at break times he was frequently to be seen on his own. His interest in schoolwork seemed to disappear and he rarely did homework. His parents wondered if he was being bullied, which he always strongly denied.

His second year in secondary school was even more difficult than the first. He never refused to go to school, but his reluctance to go was clear from the daily battle between himself and his mother, as she tried to get him up for school each day. Apart from going to school, he rarely left the house and seemed to have no interest in his personal hygiene or appearance, which was a further source of conflict at home. Things reached a head after a particularly difficult week when John's increasingly angry parents decided to have a serious talk with him. Their previously gentle, sensitive son told them to 'get out of my face' and said he would be better off dead than living this life. John's parents retreated in despair, not knowing which way to turn. John's mother felt so stressed that she went to her family doctor, initially seeking help for herself. The doctor listened to her story and asked her to bring John to see him. John's parents spent quite a while deciding how best to bring this up with John, who they knew would be very reluctant to go to the doctor. They chose the time carefully, when John was less angry and irritable than was usual for him, and together said they were worried about him and wanted him to go to the doctor for a check-up.

To their surprise John agreed and said he would go with his father. In the car on the way, John opened up to his father a little about how he was feeling and they agreed that they would talk to the doctor together.

In the remainder of this chapter we will discuss the changes in mood or behaviour that are common in depressed adolescents.

Irritability and anger

Disagreements and arguments with parents are part and parcel of adolescence, as young people develop their own views and ideas. Adolescents are often markedly intolerant of their parents and prefer the company and opinions of their friends. Most parents have an understanding of this and see it as a move toward independence and adult life. Depressed adolescents are not just intolerant, they are often intensely irritable and angry, and it is often within the family that this is most apparent. This anger, not surprisingly, leads to conflict within the family, which makes a bad situation worse. It is worth considering whether an angry, hostile, negative teenager might be depressed.

Excessive worrying

Depressed adolescents often have numerous anxieties and worries that they may or may not talk about. These often include worries that something bad is going to happen to their parents and may lead them to be afraid to go to sleep at night until parents are both safely home, or to be afraid to go to school in case something happens to their parents while they are not there.

Concern about appearance and what others think of them is part of normal adolescent behaviour, but when these concerns become overwhelming and prevent the young person from participating in life, depression should be considered.

Case history

Jenny was a confident child who enjoyed drama, sang in the school choir, and enjoyed playing 'girl bands' with her friends, when she usually took a lead role.

As adolescence approached, Jenny's parents noticed that she seemed to lose her confidence. She no longer wanted to perform, gave up drama classes,

> *dropped out of the choir and seemed to become pre-occupied with her appearance. She spent hours in front of the mirror each day, studying herself from all angles. She confided in her mother that she was fat and ugly, although to her parent's eyes she was a pretty young teenager. She rarely left the house except to go to school, getting ready to go taking several hours each morning. Reassurance from her parents about her appearance did no good and after some time they gave up trying to reassure her, becoming angry and frustrated at her self-absorption. They knew that preoccupation with appearance was normal in adolescence, but Jenny's life was overwhelmed with these concerns and they felt this could not be 'normal'.*

Fall-off in school performance

Depressed young people find it very hard to concentrate on things that require sustained mental effort. This may lead to falling grades in school, or, in conscientious perfectionistic young people, it may lead to excessive hours spent on homework which never reaches what they consider to be a good enough standard.

A dilemma for some parents is the fact that their teenagers can concentrate, often for hours on end, on computer games, which, with their rapidly changing imagery, provide constant stimulation. This often baffles and angers parents. Depressed young people sometimes explain that the computer is a form of self-therapy for them, a time when they can escape from the turmoil in their minds.

Aches and pains

Minor aches and pains are part of everyday life, and in most cases we do not dwell on them and they pass. Depressed young people often become preoccupied by aches and pains, worrying that they may have an underlying serious illness. These are not 'imaginary pains' or 'put-on pains', they are genuinely felt pains that cause huge distress to the young person, while often causing frustration and anger to parents and doctors when no physical cause can be found for them.

One teenager, David, aged 16, describes how he felt when he was depressed:

> *There's no word for it. I mean, it was akin to feeling sick. I mean, very akin to it. There were times when you'd feel physically ill at ease. Or, you know, stomach cramps or headache or something. And you'd take a series of pills for a while and that would go away, so it was very akin to being sick. Or if you were very tired all the time, there'd be suggestions to get rid of it, but they just wouldn't work. So it'd be very like an illness. I'm not sure what I'd call it though.*

Suicidal behaviour

Many research studies have shown that fleeting thoughts of suicide are common in adolescence. Such thoughts usually occur in response to a row, a broken relationship, a failure or some upset. These thoughts are usually dismissed and do not lead to suicidal behaviour.

Depressed young people frequently have not just fleeting thoughts of suicide, but may become preoccupied by such thoughts, which are constantly there, just under the surface. They may talk about death or suicide, and conversations like this should always be taken seriously. It is a myth that people who talk about suicide never carry it out. Suicide, while rare, is a common cause of death in young men in late adolescence and in their early twenties in Ireland, and is also a leading cause of death in this age group in the UK.

While suicide is thankfully rare, self-harming behaviour, such as taking an overdose of tablets or cutting one's wrists or forearms, is much more common and may be an indication of depression. Young people who cut themselves in this way are often not truly suicidal. Many explain that the pain of the cut brings temporary relief from intolerable feelings of anger, sadness or frustration. This can be seen as a warning sign that such a young person needs help, whether or not they are depressed. Please see Chapter 8 for more details of dealing with young people who self-harm or who are suicidal.

Recognising depression in your son/daughter may not be easy, but long-lasting changes in mood or behaviour that prevent your youngster from being able to get on with life, or suicidal or self-harming behaviours are very suggestive of a depressive disorder. If in doubt, trust your instincts. You know your child better than anyone else and you have his or her best interests at heart.

3

Depression in young people who already have difficulties

Depressive disorders in young people are rarely clear-cut, easy to recognise and uncomplicated. Parents who seek information in books or on the Internet about their child's difficulties will often find that the symptoms they notice seem to fit with several different conditions. For example, having a short attention span and poor concentration may be due to a physical illness, anxiety, attention deficit hyperactivity disorder (ADHD), a learning disability, an autistic spectrum disorder, drug or alcohol use and other conditions as well as depression. There is an overlap between many mental health problems in young people, such that depressive disorders often go hand in hand with other conditions. This can be very confusing to parents who want a clear answer about the nature of their child's difficulties.

Mental health professionals often spend a great deal of time at the first meeting with a young person and their family taking a full history of the young person's development and how they function in various areas of their lives. This broad picture helps them to decide which areas are causing the most difficulties, which diagnosis best fits with the young person's difficulties and where to direct treatment.

Young people who have difficulties managing their emotions or their behaviour and those with learning difficulties or with developmental problems are more prone to depression than young people who have not had these difficulties. The reasons for this are probably complex and include not only possible biological or physical vulnerabilities affecting the brain but also the negative effect on the young person's self-esteem of having long-standing difficulties, all of which makes them more prone to depression.

Any emotional or behavioural problem may be associated with an increased risk of depression, but some disorders have a more clear-cut association. Young people with learning difficulties, ADHD, oppositional defiant disorder or conduct disorder and those with Asperger's syndrome have an increased risk of developing depression in adolescence.

Learning difficulties

This may be a general learning disability affecting all areas of the young person's ability to learn, or the learning disability may be specific (e.g., a specific reading disability [dyslexia] or a specific writing disability). These disabilities pose considerable problems for young people, as they struggle on a daily basis to keep up with peers. Many such children are acutely aware of their difficulties and often have a poor self-image regarding themselves as 'thick' or 'stupid'. Children with these difficulties often receive a great deal of support and extra help in primary school, but when they move to secondary school the same level of support may not be available or the young person may refuse to avail of extra help because he or she does not want to be different from his or her peers. School can become very difficult for such young people, as they face an increasingly challenging curriculum. In adult terms, it must be a bit like having to go to work everyday to do a job that you know you cannot do properly and you know that the other people you work with can see your difficulties. It is not hard to understand how some young people manage this situation by 'acting out', becoming disruptive or aggressive, while others become withdrawn and depressed.

If your child has learning difficulties and you notice a persistent change in their behaviour, it is worth considering whether they might be depressed and taking action to support them. You can acknowledge how difficult school might be for them and seek to ensure they get the best type of educational support for their difficulties. It is also useful to help them seek out other extra-curricular activities and interests that they enjoy doing and can boost their self-esteem.

Attention deficit hyperactivity disorder (ADHD)

ADHD becomes apparent in the early years, either at the toddler stage or when the child starts school. The core features are hyperactivity, short attention span and impulsive behaviour. The condition varies from being mild, such that it presents a minor inconvenience, to being so severe that it interferes significantly with the life of the child and with family life. ADHD is often associated with learning and behaviour difficulties and with difficulties getting along with other children. It is more common in boys than in girls, and there is often a family history of similar problems. Early diagnosis and treatment can make a difference, and there are clear guidelines of treatments that work well in ADHD. These include:

- helping parents to understand the condition and how it affects their child;
- helping parents to manage their child's behaviour in a way that reduces the behavioural problems;
- social skills training (especially for older children) to help them cope with everyday situations where the ADHD gets in the way;
- medication such as methylphenidate (Ritalin or Concenta) to reduce the symptoms of ADHD.

Some young people with ADHD develop depression in adolescence. They have usually had much experience of failure, are often excluded by other children, have very low self-esteem and are in conflict with the world around them (parents, teachers, neighbours, etc.). The depression may show itself in a worsening of their behavioural difficulties, or an increase in aggressive behaviour, and may not be immediately recognisable as depression. If your child with ADHD develops such changes, he might be depressed. You should mention your concerns to the mental health professional who is looking after your child's care, as treatment for depression coexisting with ADHD can be very effective.

Case history

Don, aged 15, was diagnosed as having ADHD when he was 8. He had been in trouble at school for disrupting the class with his constant chatter and his inability to stay sitting at his table for longer than a few minutes. He had fallen behind the rest of his classmates as he rarely was able to finish a piece of work, forgot to take down notes about his homework or had lost the books necessary to do it. The other children regarded him as a source of awe and amusement in the classroom as he was always in trouble, always did the same thing again, and never seemed to mind what punishment he got. At home, things were much the same. Getting Don up and out to school required immense patience, as he could never find what he needed and was always late. His mother dreaded his return from school – he was usually in a bad mood and she knew that the battle surrounding homework lay ahead.

Understanding that Don had ADHD was a great help to his parents. They could now make sense of his difficulties. They attended a course for parents of children with ADHD, at which they learned about the importance of predictable routine, preparing in advance, breaking tasks down into small steps and avoiding lengthy arguments. A number of behavioural techniques were also useful, such as focusing on Don's positive behaviour and having small numbers of rules but with predictable consequences which were enforced if he broke the rules. Don started on Ritalin, a medication that has been shown to help children with ADHD, and his parents and teachers noticed a marked improvement in his behaviour and his ability to learn in school.

Things continued uneventfully throughout primary school and Don moved to secondary school when he was 13. By this time Don was self-conscious about having to take Ritalin and had started to 'forget' to take it. This was followed by a refusal to take it, as Don believed he didn't need it. His hyperactive behaviour had improved, but his concentration difficulties were still causing major difficulties in the classroom. Some of Don's teachers accepted the diagnosis of ADHD and made a special effort with him, while others regarded him as immature and lazy and were in constant conflict with him. Don started to play truant from school, but this was quickly spotted by the school who worked out a system of letting his parents know if he was not at school. He continued to play truant, leading to conflict between his parents and himself. Don became increasingly withdrawn at home, spending most of the time in his room. When he did go out he started to use cannabis, initially just at weekends but later regularly throughout the week. It helped him to feel relaxed and better in himself. However, even though he knew he was using too much, he could not stop. When he returned home in the early hours of the morning, there were inevitable rows with his parents who knew from his appearance and behaviour that he was using something.

Things came to a head one night when Don hit his father during a row after he had returned home at 2.30 a.m. dishevelled and with his eyes glazed. The next day, when everyone had calmed down, all three agreed that they could not continue the way they were going. Don agreed to return to see *the psychiatrist he had attended in the past with his ADHD. Don told the psychiatrist that over the past 2 years his world had 'collapsed around him'. He felt helpless and powerless and had seriously considered suicide, but held back because he could not hurt his parents in that way.*

Don's road to recovery was slow, but he was able, very gradually and with the help of his parents, to get his life back on track. He took a month off school, but met with his year head a number of times during that month to talk over how he would manage his schoolwork and his school day when he returned. He also had regular meetings with his psychiatrist, who discussed his cannabis use and how he might cut that down. Antidepressant medication was discussed, but the psychiatrist would only prescribe it when Don was able to give him a guarantee that he was no longer using cannabis. Don's parents were also involved in that decision. Don and his parents attended for family therapy, where they worked toward improving communication between them.

Don is now 16. He continues to have ups and downs in his life, but overall is making good progress. He attends an alternative course for young people who find mainstream school hard to handle. He is a regular attender and enjoys some of the subjects, such as IT, Home Economics and Woodwork, but continues to find English and Maths difficult. He is no longer depressed and has not gone back to using cannabis. He plans to do an apprenticeship in painting and decorating.

Occasionally, the possibility of ADHD springs to mind when children develop symptoms of restlessness, impulsivity, poor concentration or behavioural problems in adolescence. However, ADHD does not have its onset in adolescence, so that the appearance of these symptoms at that stage should lead to a search for other contributing factors, such as drug use or the development of depressive or anxiety disorders.

There are many books for parents of children with ADHD, such as the excellent *Taking Charge of ADHD* by Russell Barkley (for details see the 'Resources' chapter).

Conduct problems

Children with a long-standing history of behavioural or conduct problems are more prone to develop depression in adolescence than those without these difficulties. Such children are often labelled as having oppositional defiant disorder. This is the name given to a number of behaviours including persistent negative, hostile, defiant behaviour, persistent anger and resentment, temper tantrums, low frustration tolerance and disobedience, which tend to go together and have their onset in early to mid-childhood. Such children appear to be 'at odds' with the world. Conduct disorder is the name given to the more serious degree of behavioural difficulties, where the young person infringes the rights of others and the rules of society and is involved in such activities as theft, bullying, cruelty to people or animals, assault and destructiveness.

Although conduct problems usually have their onset in early to mid-childhood as already mentioned, they can become apparent for the first time in adolescence. The outlook for young people with untreated conduct disorder is poor, in that they are at increased risk of social and mental health problems. Because of this, every effort should be made to provide help to these young people and to address the problems. Things that can help are extra-consistent parenting that helps these young people learn responsibility, educational programmes that address their particular needs and social skills training that build on their strengths. Because of the stress of managing behavioural problems, parents need every support in dealing with these challenging difficulties. In addition, some young people with conduct problems have an underlying depressive disorder that contributes in a major way to their behavioural difficulties, and this possibility should be explored with any young person with behavioural difficulties. This is easier said than done, as many of these young people are angry and hostile, have limited ability to express in words what they are feeling inside and feel very threatened by adults trying to find out what's going on in their minds. However, it is important to address their emotional needs in this way if possible, and it can be a welcome relief for them, making a change from being constantly in trouble because of their behaviour. The long-term aim is to help them express their feelings and to help them take responsibility for their behaviour.

Asperger's syndrome

Asperger's syndrome is a developmental disorder that most people believe is a mild form of autism. Children with Asperger's syndrome are usually intelligent but have a combination of social skills deficits, an unusual conversational style and intense particular interests, which make them very different from other children.

They have great difficulty in appreciating or understanding the feelings of other people or the effects of their behaviour on others. Their understanding of language is very concrete and they do not readily appreciate subtlety or irony. Their use of language is often quite distinctive, engaging in long, one-sided conversations without noticing the effects of their conversation on the listener. Their language is often complicated and formal, using long words and is often more 'adult' than you would expect from a child of their age. They sometimes have an unusual intonation to their speech − it may be flat and monotonous or sometimes they have an accent that does not fit in with their cultural or social background. As already mentioned, one feature of children with Asperger's syndrome is their tendency to have a number of special interests, which they pursue intensely and in which they may become quite expert.

Asperger's syndrome can range from very mild, when it passes almost unnoticed and the child is just regarded as a little bit 'odd', to very severe, where the child's difficulties make him stand out from other children. It is likely we all know adults with undiagnosed Asperger's syndrome, as this diagnosis has only been made with any degree of regularity in recent years, although the condition was first described over 50 years ago.

Children with Asperger's syndrome who grow up with informed, caring parents and teachers often get through primary school without too much difficulty. Some of these children do not seem to feel the lack of friends and enjoy their relationships with family and other adults who are intrigued by their unusual ways, while other children with Asperger's syndrome are acutely aware of their lack of friends and their difficulties fitting in with other children and long for things to be different. Adolescence can be a very lonely time for these young people. It is the stage in life when the need to be seen as the same as your peers is at its greatest. Many long to be accepted by their peers but do not have the social skills for this to happen.

Depression in young people with Asperger's syndrome may be easy to recognise with a change in mood, sleep and appetite patterns, but often it is not that clear-cut. Rather, the young person's depression may show itself as increased anger or hostility, or by increasingly withdrawn behaviour. It can be very difficult for young people who have Asperger's syndrome to put into words what they are feeling, and they may reject the idea that they are depressed. The help of an experienced mental health professional can be very useful in both the diagnosis of depression in adolescents with Asperger's syndrome and in providing effective treatment. Antidepressant medication is often helpful, but energy needs to be put into trying to do something about the underlying causes, which for adolescents with Asperger's syndrome is often an awareness of their differences from other people. There are different views about whether it is in the best interests of a child with Asperger's syndrome to tell him or her of the diagnosis and when this should be done. If the child is asking why he or she is different and is troubled by this, it is probably helpful for him or her to be given information about the diagnosis in a sensitive way. There are now many books and websites for young people with Asperger's syndrome, which can help them to communicate with each other and to feel connected to a community of other young people with similar difficulties.

Case history

John, aged 9, was referred by his school to his local child and adolescent mental health service because he was having great difficulty mixing with other children. His main interests in life were wildlife and dinosaurs, and he talked about these incessantly. Other children avoided him, which he could not understand. He began to develop stomach pains and complained of feeling sick on school mornings, and it was very difficult for his parents to get him to attend. John was an only child with very supportive parents, who were aware of his unusual interests, his need for routine and predictability in his life and his difficulties with social interaction. Following assessment, John was diagnosed as having Asperger's syndrome and his parents were given a great deal of information about the condition. They were encouraged to join a support group for parents of children with Asperger's syndrome, and the psychologist showed them how to work with John at home using reading and storytelling to help him to learn how to handle common social situations. The school was also very understanding and arranged special support for John from a resource teacher, who spent time with him every day, sometimes on his own, sometimes in small groups, helping him with the subjects he found difficult and also working to develop his social skills.

John was referred again when he was 14 and in his second year at secondary school. He had found the move from primary to secondary school very difficult and once again had developed stomach pains and nausea on school mornings, and getting him up for school was a daily battle. He was adamant that he hated school and that he wanted to leave. Reports from his school described John as not mixing at all with peers, not functioning in class and spending his break time on his own either reading or walking around the playground talking to himself. At home he had become increasingly angry, sometimes with explosions of anger that invariably ended in tears. He spent most of his time in his room and was not taking care of his personal hygiene. His relationship with his parents, which had previously been warm and close, was very strained, and they were worried that he might harm himself, as they had witnessed the depths of his distress and felt powerless to help him.

Following assessment where a diagnosis of depressive disorder complicating his Asperger's syndrome was made, a plan to help John was put in place. John was referred to an adolescent day treatment programme but was very reluctant to attend. Following negotiation, he agreed to attend initially for 1 hour each day. This was gradually increased over a 6-week period until he was attending for full days. The day programme had a teacher who was very experienced with adolescents with a range of mental health problems. She worked with John, initially on an individual basis but later within the classroom at the day unit. John was treated with antidepressant medication and his mood gradually improved and he become less agitated and anxious.

John's parents and the staff in the day programme gave a lot of thought about whether or not it would be helpful to tell John of his diagnosis of Asperger's syndrome. On the one hand, they felt he had a right to know, that it would help him to understand his difficulties better and would open up a channel of communication for him with other young people with Asperger's syndrome. On the other hand, they knew that John's greatest fear was that 'there is something wrong with me', and they worried how a diagnosis of Asperger's syndrome might confirm that view.

Following much deliberation, they decided it was best to tell him. They felt it would be best if his parents did this. His parents told him that they had been doing a lot of research about how best to help him and had found this book about Asperger's syndrome which they thought he might find interesting. (There are now a number of books written by young people with Asperger's syndrome for young people with the condition.) John read the book but spoke little about it, and when his parents asked him what he thought of it he said it was 'a bit weird' and made it clear he did not want to discuss it further.

John is now 16 and is attending an alternative school, where he takes seven subjects, goes in for his classes and leaves when they are over. The school is aware of his difficulties and does not put pressure on him to socialise. He remains socially isolated but is no longer depressed, angry and troubled. His parents feel that, as he gets older, he will probably find his niche in the world, and they hope he will meet like-minded people and will understand himself a bit better.

Conclusion

Many children who are depressed also have other long-standing problems, such as learning difficulties, ADHD, conduct problems and Asperger's syndrome. These difficulties can contribute to a child feeling depressed, especially as he or she approaches adolescence. Managing depression in young people who have these difficulties can be a great challenge, but parents of these young people will have had a great deal of experience of dealing with challenges. Many of the ideas in this book are useful for parents of such children, but as change can be slow, even more patience might be needed.

4

Could it be due to something else?

Parents who are coping with a child who is depressed often wonder whether this could be the start of some other mental illness. 'Depressed' often seems to be too mild a term to describe the changes they observe in their child. A number of conditions can be associated with depression, and others have symptoms that may be hard to distinguish from depression. It is no wonder that parents sometimes feel confused.

Some of the conditions parents worry about include:

- effects of alcohol;
- effects of drugs;
- a serious physical illness;
- sexual abuse;
- schizophrenia;
- eating disorders;
- bipolar affective disorder (manic depressive disorder).

Is it due to alcohol?

The relationship between depression and alcohol is a complicated one. There is no doubt that excessive use of alcohol can cause fatigue, loss of energy and depression. In our culture, people often drink enormous quantities at weekends (binge-drinking) and abstain during the week. This can lead to highs and lows of mood with irritability and depression being the norm from Monday to Thursday, with alcohol-induced 'highs' happening over the weekend. This pattern of drinking, which often starts in mid-adolescence, may only happen on special occasions to begin with, but may gradually become a way of life. This may happen with any young person whose drinking starts to take on a life of its own. These young people are often very defensive about their drinking and will usually deny that it is causing any problem, but you, as a parent, will know how much of a problem it is causing in the household. The young person will usually point to their abstinence during the week as evidence that they can control their drinking.

Some young people who are suffering from depression use alcohol as a form of 'self-medication'. It helps them to relax, gives them confidence and makes them feel one of the group. Using alcohol in small amounts can have these positive effects, but young people rarely limit their drinking to small amounts and what started out as a helpful boost may become something that adds to their problems and makes their depression worse.

If your child is drinking in the ways described above, there is a problem. You should try to talk over your concerns with him and ask him if there is any way you can help him to cut down on his alcohol use. Though this may be ineffective, at least your child will be aware of your concerns. It may be that, without realising it, you are facilitating your child's drinking by providing the money, writing excuse notes for school or ringing his or her place of work to explain absences. It is very understandable that you would want to protect your child in this way, but it does not work in the long term. There may come a time when you have to directly confront the drinking and insist that your child comes with you to seek help. It is a good idea to have found out in advance what services are available and to have contacted them for advice about how best to approach your child. Your family doctor or local social services department will be able to advise on local services.

It is also worth considering what sort of message your child is getting from the attitudes of other family members to alcohol and how they use it. There is often a family history of alcohol problems in young people who use alcohol in a problematic way. Some of this may be due to a genetic influence, but it is likely that the child also learns from what he or she observes. If the young person grows up in surroundings where excessive use of alcohol is seen as a way of celebrating, commiserating or dealing with upset and anger, then it is not surprising if they do the same.

Could it be due to drugs?

Virtually all teenagers are exposed to street drugs which are widely available in most communities and in all social groups. We know from numerous surveys that the majority of young people experiment with 'soft' drugs, such as cannabis, which they say helps them to relax, does not have such unpleasant side effects as nausea and aggression that alcohol can have and which they regard as safe.

Occasional use of cannabis by a healthy young person probably has few ill effects. The problems occur when it is used by depressed young persons as a way of treating their depression. The only time they may feel 'OK' is when they are under the influence of cannabis. Many depressed young people tell us how easy it is to get into the habit of relaxing with cannabis and how hard it is to break this habit. Regular excessive use of cannabis can make depression worse and can lead to a loss of motivation or drive, which is very like depression. Sometimes it is impossible to know which is the chicken and which is the egg – is the cannabis use causing depression or is the depression leading to excessive use of cannabis?

If your child is spending a lot of money with little to show for it, staying out very late or not coming home at night and returning home in a somewhat 'mind-altered' state, you have good reason to be concerned about possible drug use. It is worth trying to find ways to talk to him about it when you are both calm. Getting angry, blaming and 'laying down the law' is unlikely to be helpful, despite your understandable fears. Services vary from area to area – your family doctor or local social services department will be able to advise you about what services are available and how to arrange an appointment.

A serious physical illness

Young people with severe depression can often look unwell or ill and may complain of numerous physical symptoms, such as headaches, aches and pains, poor appetite and tiredness. It is not surprising that parents often wonder if their child might have an undiagnosed physical problem. Indeed, the depressed young person often fears this as well.

Depression in young people may be associated with physical illness – this is unusual, but it can happen. Sometimes depression starts after a viral illness, a bad bout of flu or glandular fever. This type of 'post-viral depression' may last weeks to months. Rare physical conditions, such as hypothyroidism or disorders of the adrenal glands, may lead to mood changes and depression and very occasionally brain tumours may present in this way. The psychiatrist who is assessing your child will have these conditions in mind and will arrange the necessary medical investigations if these are indicated. Depression in young people is rarely due to an undiagnosed physical disorder, but if you or your child have concerns about this it is important to mention them to the psychiatrist.

Sexual abuse

When a previously happy child becomes withdrawn, irritable, angry and secretive, parents often wonder if something could have happened to them and sexual abuse may come to mind. There is much more openness about discussing sexual abuse nowadays, but it is still common for children who have been abused not to tell anyone about it until they reach adult life. There are many reasons why young people may not tell – they may have been threatened by the abuser, they may not wish to get the abuser into trouble, they may fear that they have done something wrong or will be blamed or they may fear the reaction of their parents.

If you have concerns that your child has been sexually abused, it is important to try to find a way to talk to her about it. It may help to introduce the topic with something like 'I was thinking about how down in yourself you seem to be lately and I was wondering if anything could have happened to upset you – something like being bullied or sexually abused or having a bad experience?' By stating your concerns in this way, you are avoiding putting them in a situation were they feel under pressure to respond one way or another. If you can mention your concerns in a calm way, it may give your child the confidence they need to tell you if they have been abused. By mentioning sexual abuse as a possibility along with other difficult experiences, you are giving your child a message that this is something that can be talked about, that is not so bad that it cannot be mentioned.

If you have concerns that your child may have been sexually abused, but are worried about discussing this possibility with her, it may be a good idea to talk over your concerns with a close friend or a professional. Your family doctor will probably know who is the most appropriate professional in your area or your local social services department may be able to advise.

Schizophrenia

Schizophrenia is a serious mental illness, which often has its onset in late adolescence. It affects about one person in every hundred, and there may be a history of schizophrenia in relatives or other family members. It causes serious changes in the young person's functioning and affects their thinking, their emotions, how they experience the world and their ability to relate to other people. It can come to light in a number of ways. Some young people with schizophrenia become progressively more withdrawn or 'odd' over several months or years, while others develop more acute symptoms, such as delusions (where they develop fixed false beliefs that are not shared by other people in their community and that they hold with firm conviction) or hallucinations (where they experience a sensation in the absence of any external sources for that sensation).

The delusions are often 'paranoid' in type, in which the young person believes that others are out to get him or harm him or involve feeling controlled by an outside source, and can be very frightening.

The hallucinations often involve hearing 'voices' talking about the person or giving a running commentary on their behaviour. They may say very derogatory things about the person which are highly upsetting.

There are new effective treatments for schizophrenia, involving medication, various forms of therapy and rehabilitation programmes. Research has clearly shown that the outlook is best when treatment is started early.

Young people with schizophrenia often become depressed, and it can be hard in many cases to be clear as to whether the young person's symptoms are mainly due to a severe depressive disorder or schizophrenia. Sometimes it is only the passage of time and the response to treatment that makes this clear, even to an experienced psychiatrist.

If your child's depressive disorder has features that make you worry that it might be schizophrenia, do discuss your concerns with the mental health team involved in your child's care. In many cases they will be able to reassure you that your child does not have schizophrenia and, where they are uncertain themselves, they will be open with you about it.

Eating disorders

Eating disorders, such as anorexia nervosa and bulimia, are not uncommon and can be difficult to separate from 'ordinary' depression at times, as young people with eating disorders often have accompanying depression. Anorexia nervosa frequently starts in early to mid-adolescence and occurs mainly in girls, but boys can also be affected. In anorexia there is an intense fear of fatness and a relentless pursuit of thinness, in which the young person restricts their food intake leading to weight loss that may reach a dangerous level. They become consumed by their desire to be thin, such that these pre-occupations occupy much of their lives. Their thinking is often distorted, in that they see themselves as 'fat', while others see a skeletal figure.

Depression is quite common in anorexia nervosa, and parents of young people, especially girls with depression and weight loss, are often concerned about the possibility of anorexia nervosa. The weight loss that sometimes occurs in 'ordinary' depressive disorders is due to loss of appetite, rather than consciously restricting food intake, and is generally not particularly welcomed by the young person who often feels very unwell and lacking in energy.

If you are the parent of a young person who is losing weight for no apparent reason, you are right to be concerned. Your child should have a medical check-up, and the doctor will be able to advise on what further help is necessary.

Bulimia is probably fairly common, and as it does not have the outward signs of dramatic weight loss that occur in anorexia nervosa, it can be a hidden problem. Bulimia involves episodes of binge-eating, in which the young person eats vast quantities of food and then takes steps to avoid weight gain by engaging in self-induced vomiting, misuse of laxatives or excessive exercise. These cycles of behaviour may happen infrequently or up to several times a day in severe cases of bulimia. Young people with bulimia are usually very unhappy and guilty about their behaviour, and depression is quite common.

Eating disorders are ways in which young people who are in emotional turmoil try to deal with their problems by focusing on food, weight and shape. It can seem to others that the young person is being deliberately self-destructive, while the young person sees it as their means of survival. If you are concerned that your child has an eating disorder, talk over your concerns with your family doctor or try one of the helplines listed in 'Resources' at the end of the book. It can be difficult to persuade young people with eating disorders to get help for themselves, but with patience and determination most parents succeed with this task.

Bipolar affective disorder (manic depressive disorder)

This may be of concern to parents, particularly if there is a family history of bipolar affective disorder. The main feature of bipolar disorder is extreme changes of mood, involving periods of being elated, overactive, overtalkative, euphoric and speeded up when 'high' or hypomanic, and periods of being slowed down, miserable, sad, guilty, hopeless, lacking in energy, even suicidal when 'low' or depressed. These mood changes may happen over periods of weeks, months or years, and the person may have long periods of normal or stable moods in between mood swings. In some young people with bipolar affective disorder, the mood swings can happen very rapidly, over hours, or the young person can have some features of being 'high' and some of being 'low' at the same time. These mood changes can have a very damaging effect on relationships with other people, on school and work life and on the person's self-confidence. Early recognition and treatment can prevent some of these other problems from developing.

Bipolar affective disorder may start with a depressive episode that is indistinguishable from 'ordinary' depression. This may be followed months or years later by an upswing of mood where the person is 'high' or hypomanic.

Mood-stabilizing medication, such as carbamazapine, sodium valproate or lithium, can greatly reduce the mood swings, and information and education about the disorder can help young persons manage their lifestyle in a way that reduces the risk of mood swings. It may not be possible until time has passed to tell the difference between 'ordinary' depression and the start of bipolar affective disorder. Parents should talk over their concerns with the psychiatrist treating their child.

The Manic Depression Fellowship has very useful information and education programmes for those with bipolar affective disorder and for family members – see 'Resources' at the end of the book.

While many depressive disorders in young people are clear-cut with little doubt about the diagnosis, other young people may have a mixture of symptoms and may appear to have features of some of the above disorders. This can be a source of enormous anxiety to parents, who should avail themselves of all the support that is provided by the mental health team involved with their child.

5

Getting help

Parents of a depressed child often feel helpless and doubt if anything can be done to improve the situation. This same feeling is common in family members trying to help a depressed person of any age. It is as if the depression is in some way 'contagious', spreading out to engulf those closest to the depressed person. Recognising there is a problem is a major first step, and here it is important to trust your own 'gut feeling' as a parent. If your young person has the features of depression mentioned in Chapter 2 and you believe they are depressed, this is often a hugely positive step forward.

You may however be unsure if they are depressed – maybe it is just teenage moodiness or a difficult phase they are going through. It is often useful to talk to other people who know your child well, to get their view on how your child is doing.

Other people may see your child in a different light and may have information which can help you assess the situation more clearly.

Talking to others who know your child

Parents are often reluctant to do this, feeling a sense of
disloyalty to their child or fearing 'airing the family's dirty
linen' in public. But it can be done in a way that is not
disloyal. You can say something like 'we are a bit worried
about Kevin, he just does not seem to be himself at home
recently. How have you found him?' There may be a close
relative who knows your child well, and it is always worth
talking to your child's teacher or school guidance counsellor. This will give you useful information. It may be
that your child's mood and behaviour have not changed in
other settings, such as at school or with friends. This
makes a depressive disorder less likely, although it does
not rule it out, as many depressed young people are very
careful not to show how they are feeling to their friends or
at school. If, on the other hand, your child's teacher has
noticed a change, this opens up the possibility of further
discussion: is he mixing well, is he participating in class, is
it possible he is being bullied?

Help within the family

It is encouraging to know that not all depressed teenagers
need specialised help. There is much that can be done by
parents and family members. It is well worth taking a
close look at the family as it may appear to your child.
Parents are generally well aware of the impact on a
young person of parental separation or divorce, but may
not be as aware of the impact of long-standing marital
conflict or serious heavy drinking. You, as a parent, may

have learned to live with such problems, but your child may not. Dealing with such problems is never easy, but recognising that they may be contributing to your child's depression may give you the courage and energy to take the first step.

Is it possible that all the demands on you as a modern busy parent have left little time or energy for communication with your teenager? Adolescents are often intensely lonely, as they struggle to become independent of their parents and part of a longed-for peer group. Sometimes taking steps to help yourself be calmer as a parent and to have more time can open up communication with a troubled teenager.

How the family can help is dealt with more fully in Chapter 7.

Finding out what help is available

In many situations the steps mentioned above may be enough to help your child to be less depressed – this is particularly so in mild to moderate depressive disorders. If your child remains depressed, it is a good idea to find out what services are available in your area to help. Your family doctor will be aware of the services that are available locally that might be most useful to you and your child. Sometimes family doctors are able to establish a good relationship with a depressed young person, and many cases of adolescent depression are dealt with in this way. If your family doctor does not feel she or he is the right person, she or he may suggest referral to either counselling or to a child and adolescent mental health service.

Tom's story

(continued from page 10)

Tom's mother discusses her concerns with his father. He is inclined to view Tom's behaviour as due to laziness and feels he needs the modern-day equivalent of a 'kick in the pants'. He has tried this approach in the past, but it has not worked. He tries again – giving Tom a good 'talking to', demanding that he be more polite to the family and that he gets up for school each day. He is not there to enforce this, as he leaves for work at 7 a.m., and Tom's mother cannot enforce it either. Tom's behaviour gets worse – now he has stopped going to school, saying he is too tired.

Tom's parents discuss the situation further. They cannot understand why Tom, who was an active boy until 2 years ago, should have become so tired and 'lazy'. They decide to take him to the doctor for a check-up. Tom's mother picks a time when Tom is calm (and so is she) and suggests that he should have a check-up with their family doctor. He is not at all keen to go, but agrees reluctantly when his mother says they need to find out why he is so tired.

(continued on p. 57)

Counselling

If your young person is able to talk about his or her problems and is willing to get help, counselling or psychotherapy may be useful. Some general practices have counsellors as part of the service they provide and many large towns and cities now have teen counselling services. Many schools have guidance counsellors who may be another useful resource.

Child and adolescent mental health services

Within Ireland and the UK, Child and Adolescent Mental Health Services (CAMHSs) operate on a 'catchment area' basis and provide a free service to young people and their families living in their geographical catchment area. Your family doctor will know about these services, and will discuss referral with you, if this seems appropriate. CAMHSs usually involve a team of professionals, including child and adolescent psychiatrists, psychologists, social workers, psychotherapists and others. Referral to such services is particularly useful if your child's depression is complicated: when there are other emotional, behavioural or family problems; when risk of suicide is a major concern, or when your child's depression has not responded to the steps you have already taken.

Many CAMHSs have long waiting lists, but operate a system of prioritising referrals when there is risk to the health or life of the young person. If you have real concerns that your child may be suicidal or if his or her depression is affecting his or her physical health (e.g., if they are not eating or drinking sufficiently), you should ask your doctor to request an urgent appointment. Once the referral has been made, you can always make contact yourself with the CAMHS Clinic, to make your concerns clear and to find out when it is likely you will get an appointment.

Communicating with your teenager about the need for further help

This may be quite difficult. Young people rarely recognise depression in themselves and almost never ask for help. This is partly due to the way depression affects their thinking, such that they cannot see how anything could help them to feel better, and partly because of the understandable reluctance many young people feel about discussing their private fears and concerns with other people.

It is a good idea to carefully plan how best to broach the topic of getting further help with your teenager. If both parents can agree on the need for further help and can support their child through this process, that is the ideal situation. Often this is not possible. It is common for parents to have quite different views on their child's problems or parents may have difficulties in their own communication, making this a difficult area to discuss.

It is best to discuss your child's problems with the other parent when you are both calm. Try to do it without blaming each other and keep in mind that both of you, as parents, care deeply about your child and want what is best for him. If you disagree, it is unlikely to be because either of you does not care, rather that you have different views on how best to help. Differences such as these may need many conversations to get sorted out. Try to listen to the views of your spouse/partner/ex-partner. Maybe she or he has an idea for helping your child that differs from your own, but is worth trying. The need for professional help may become more obvious if other ways of helping have not improved the situation.

Tom's story

(continued from page 54)

Tom's family doctor talks to Tom's mother first and then sees Tom on his own. She gives him a physical check-up and, while doing this, asks him a few questions about how things are going with his friends, school and football, which Tom used to play but no longer does. Tom talks a little to the doctor, saying he doesn't have any friends, does not want to play football and has not been going to school. In response to the doctor's low-key questions, Tom says that he is feeling awful and does not know why. He tells the doctor he has been thinking of suicide a lot and cannot get it out of his mind.

The doctor tells Tom that his physical check-up has not shown any medical problem that could explain how he is feeling. She suggests to Tom that it would be a good idea to go to see someone who might be able to help him with the difficult feelings he's been having. She does not label Tom's experience as 'depression' as she is not sure herself if that is what it is and she also knows that boys of Tom's age are often very reluctant to accept that label. Tom reluctantly agrees to the doctor's suggestion.

(continued on p. 73)

Approaching your depressed child

Again, pick your time carefully, when you are both calm and not rushed or angry. Don't ask your child how he is feeling – he will probably say 'fine' angrily or defensively ask you why you want to know. It's better to mention specific concerns you have, such as 'I'm worried about you because you are always in your room and you seem upset a lot of the time.' Don't get drawn into an argument about whether or not he is spending a lot of time in his room – just try to keep yourself calm and say that you feel that you all need some help to sort things out and that you have made an appointment with (named person) to see if they can help.

Younger children will generally co-operate with this approach, but it may be more difficult with adolescents. If you are calm, positive and determined, most will agree eventually, having initially said no. Most adolescents, while angry and defensive on the surface, want their parents to recognise their distress and will reluctantly co-operate with getting further help. There is a section 'He won't go for help' in Chapter 9 that may be useful if, despite your best efforts, your child will not agree to seek further help.

Case history

Stephen, aged 15, lives with his mother from Monday to Friday and spends the weekends, along with his two younger sisters, with his father. His parents separated 2 years ago, following several years of bitter marital rows and conflict. Both his parents are slowly making new lives for themselves.

Both have worked hard to allow the children to have a good relationship with each of them, and they believe that things are better now for the children than they have been for many years.

For Stephen, things do not appear that way at all. He is angry with his father, who he sees as leaving home and leaving him. He has not been able to talk to his father about this and is distant and withdrawn in his father's company. Many times he does not want to go to his father for the weekend – he misses his friends and has to spend long hours with his younger sisters. He feels guilty about not wanting to spend time with his father.

Stephen becomes increasingly irritable and bad-tempered. His relationship with his mother deteriorates, as he will do almost nothing to help at home and any request results in rows and shouting. He finds he cannot talk to his friends and starts spending most of his time out of the house, walking around on his own and trying to think. One night he does not come home. His mother is beside herself with worry, as she knows this is not his usual behaviour. She phones his father, who agrees to go and look for Stephen. He finds him sitting on the canal bank, near his home. Stephen can give no explanation, except to say he was 'thinking'. He returns home with his father without protest.

The following day, Stephen's parents meet to discuss their concerns. Both have noticed changes in Stephen – he has become much quieter, seems angry much of the time and does not really talk to either of them. Both had thought that he was upset by their separation and with time would get used to it and would be more like his old self. They now realise that over the past 2 years, rather than improving he has become much quieter and more withdrawn. Finding him on his own at the canal bank in the early hours of the morning was a huge shock for them, and they both wonder what was going through his mind. They worry about the possibility of suicide. They agree that he needs professional help, but have no idea how to go about getting it.

Stephen's mother talks to their family doctor, who has known the family for many years and has treated Stephen's father for depression in the past. He suggests referral to the local CAMHS. Stephen's parents agree that this is the best course of action. They decide that Stephen's mother will discuss it with him and will tell him that she and his father have talked about it.

Stephen's mother picks a good time to talk to him. She tells him that she and his father are worried by his being so withdrawn and spending so much time 'thinking'. She says she wonders what he is thinking about, but does not ask him directly. To her surprise, Stephen opens up in a way he has not done for several years and tells her that he has been thinking of killing himself over the past several months and that he cannot get these thoughts out of his head. He seems relieved to have told her. Stephen's mother, despite feeling overwhelmed inside with fear and pity for her son's distress, responds calmly and positively. She says that she is glad he has told her how he feels and that she knows that he can be helped to not feel so sad and despairing. She tells him that they are going to go to a local clinic that helps young people who are feeling like he does. She says that both his parents will go with him, or just one of them if he would prefer that. Stephen says he would like to go with his mother for the first visit and maybe with his father for a later visit. His mother indicates that she thinks he is very courageous to deal with his problems in such a responsible way.

6

Treatment of depression

The treatment of depressive disorders in young people depends on the level of severity. Not all depressed young people need 'treatment' – many can be helped a great deal by talking to someone about how they are feeling. This may be to a parent, but adolescents often find it easier to talk to someone other than a parent – maybe a relative or family friend that they know and like. Adolescent boys find it particularly difficult to talk about their feelings, and many are helped over their depression by the interest and support of a parent, relative or family friend who 'keeps an eye out' for them, checks in with them regularly about how things are going, shows an interest in their interests and generally shows them that they care about them, without swamping them with attention or forcing them to talk.

There is no miracle cure for depression in young people, but a number of treatment approaches have been shown to be effective.

Multiple approaches

There is no single treatment for depressive disorders – in most cases a combination of treatment approaches are used. This usually involves help for the young person and for the family, to enable them to support the young person through their depression.

Therapeutic help for the young person

This generally involves some form of psychotherapy, which may take place through individual work with the young person or work in groups. There are many different forms of psychotherapy, and research has shown that the relationship that the young person forms with the therapist, 'the therapeutic relationship', is more important than the type of psychotherapy used in predicting a good outcome. All forms of psychotherapy involve regular, frequent meetings between the young person and the therapist, where the time they spend together is special time for the young person.

People often imagine that psychotherapy involves lying on a couch with a silent therapist who analyses all you say or makes assumptions about what you don't say. This is far from the reality of psychotherapy as practised with young people in Ireland and the UK. Psychotherapy with young people in our culture is very practically based, deals with real life problems and involves the young person and therapist sitting down and working together in an active way to help the young person to understand his or her stresses and conflicts better and to find healthy ways of managing them.

All forms of psychotherapy involve a confidential relationship between the young person and the therapist, but you should expect a regular meeting with your child's therapist to discuss progress. This also offers you, as a parent, the opportunity to find out if the therapist feels there are any important aspects of your family life or your relationship with your child that you need to work on. Your child's therapist will have explained to you and your child at the start of therapy that she or he will not keep confidential any concerns she or he has about your child being at serious risk, such as whether your child is suicidal, being abused or engaging in behaviour that puts her at significant risk. As a parent, you need to know if such risks are present, and the confidential nature of the relationship between your child and her therapist does not include keeping this type of information confidential.

A form of psychotherapy called cognitive behavioural therapy or CBT has been found to be an effective treatment for depressive disorders in young people. It involves regular (weekly or fortnightly) meetings between young persons and their therapist, usually over a period of somewhere between 12 and 20 weeks, sometimes followed by 'booster sessions' at 3-monthly intervals over the next 6 months to a year. CBT involves the therapist helping the young person to understand how depression can make people think and behave in a way that tends to make depression worse and gradually to try new approaches to difficult situations. It is a type of therapy that many young people enjoy, as it is very practical, not at all intimidating and deals with problem areas that they have identified.

Case history

Sue, aged 15, attended a psychotherapist for 6 weeks due to her feeling very low and depressed. She found it hard to open up at first, but when she began to trust the therapist it became a lot easier. The big thing that helped was the therapist reassuring her that coming to therapy did not mean she was 'mad' or 'mental' and that she was not to blame for her depression.

The therapist helped Sue realise the vicious cycle of depression she was caught in: she would feel low and decide not to go out and avoid going to school; not going out would make her feel bad about herself, that she was a failure; these negative thoughts would make her feel more depressed and less able to get out of the house. The therapist began to help Sue break the cycle of these negative thoughts and actions. He showed her ways of interrupting the negative thoughts of failure and helped her focus on more positive ways of viewing things. He helped her set small goals, such as 'going out for a walk' or making sure to meet a friend, and encouraged her when she did this. He helped her stop 'giving herself a hard time' when she had a setback that made her feel more depressed. Instead, he helped her be more forgiving and say 'Well, I didn't go out today, but I will try again tomorrow.' The six weeks of therapy helped Sue make some positive changes.

(continued on p. 68)

Parent support

Living with a depressed family member is difficult, and often relationships are very strained by the time families seek help. Parents may feel they have caused their young person to be depressed, but this is very rarely the case. The causes of depressive disorders in young people are complex and almost never involve one single cause. However, parents are vitally important in helping their child through depression and in helping the other children in the family (who often feel angry and resentful at what they see as 'special treatment' for the depressed child).

Recognising the importance of parents in helping young people overcome depression, many professional services offer parents support in the form of individual meetings. These meetings focus on helping parents understand the nature of their young person's depression, on identifying what they can do to help and on helping parents personally cope with a difficult situation. Sometimes this support is offered via a parenting group, as many parents find it extremely useful to meet other parents who are dealing with or who have dealt with similar problems to themselves. This can help them feel they are not alone and give them practical ideas on how to cope.

Family therapy

Family therapy involves a therapist seeing the parents with the young person in a family meeting. Depending on the needs of the family these meetings can include other family members, such as brothers and sisters and even grandparents.

Family therapy helps with relationships and communication in the family as a whole. The aim is to help parents and young people communicate better with each other and to better understand each other's experiences and feelings. It can sound a bit daunting and it can be difficult to persuade adolescents or other family members to attend, as they often fear they will be the centre of attention or will be blamed or forced to talk when they don't want to. If reluctant family members can be persuaded to attend just one session, they are usually pleasantly surprised by the relaxed, fair and positive way in which the sessions are conducted by the therapist. There are many different types of family therapy, but most aim to discover and use the strengths the family has to help the young person move on from depression.

Case history

(continued from p. 66)

In addition to attending psychotherapy, Sue also attended a number of family meetings at the clinic with her parents. The focus of the meetings was on helping Sue and her parents understand each other's point of view. Though the parents were greatly concerned about Sue's depression and wanted her to get better, some of the things they were doing weren't helpful. For example, hoping to cheer Sue up, the mother used to change the subject anytime Sue talked about negative feelings. This left Sue feeling unheard and irritable. In addition, trying to get Sue to school in the mornings involved both parents nagging and arguing with her, which led to a row leaving everyone upset.

Through the family meetings Sue and her parents learnt to do things differently. Her parents agreed to spend some time being sensitive to and

> *listening to Sue's negative feelings as well as setting up times to do more positive things to take their mind off the problems. They also agreed the morning routine about Sue getting up and going to school, which involved Sue taking more responsibility. Above all, the meetings helped Sue and her parents appreciate each other's feelings and point of view. Sue appreciated her parents concern for her, their desire to help and how difficult the depression was for them too, while her parents appreciated how difficult it was for Sue and how much support she needed.*

Medication

Antidepressant medication is sometimes recommended for treatment of moderate or severe forms of depression in teenagers. Such medications are usually used in combination with other forms of therapy, such as psychotherapy or family work. The results of these combined approaches are better than using medication alone.

Parents often feel daunted when antidepressant medication is suggested. They wonder if this is the start of a 'slippery slope', leading to a lifetime of being on medication. Antidepressant medication is generally recommended for relatively long periods, 6 months to a year in many cases. This will be closely monitored by the doctor who prescribes the medication and will be discontinued, usually gradually over a few months, after this time. If antidepressant medication is given for very short periods (e.g., for just a few weeks), it may be effective, but the depressive symptoms often return quite quickly when it is stopped. This is much less likely when the medication

is given for 6 months to a year and then discontinued
gradually.

One of the main benefits of antidepressant medication
is that it often lifts the mood of a depressed young person
enough for them to be able to get involved in some form
of talking therapy. Very depressed teenagers are often
unable to participate in psychotherapy or counselling
because their world view is so bleak that they cannot see
the point, or they cannot express how they feel in words.

Antidepressants are not 'magic pills', but they can
greatly help a young person with moderate to severe depression. The antidepressants used most often nowadays
are called SSRIs (selective serotonin reuptake inhibitors).
They are taken just once a day and in general have few
side effects. It is important to ask the doctor what the
side effects are and what to do if they happen. Most
antidepressants take 2–3 weeks to start having an effect,
and it is often 4–6 weeks before their full effect is apparent.

A great deal is made in the media of the risk of some of
the SSRIs being addictive. In practice, it is highly
unusual for young people to become dependent on
antidepressant medication. The opposite is usually the
case – most need encouragement to stay on them for a
sufficiently long time. The risk of dependence seems to
be less if they are reduced very gradually and stopped over
a period of a few months.

There is also controversy as to whether or not SSRIs
induce some people to commit suicide. Professionals are
split on this, with each side producing evidence to support
their case. It is not clear-cut, particularly as many young
people with depressive disorders for whom antidepressants are being recommended will have had definite and
often serious suicidal thoughts and intentions. Concern
about suicide is never far from the mind of a parent of a
young person with depression. This is dealt with in more
detail in Chapter 8.

Some of the SSRIs are not suitable for young people, while others are more gentle in their effects and seem to suit them better. It is important for parents to talk with the doctor who has recommended antidepressant medication for their young person and to discuss any concerns they may have. In my experience, antidepressant medication, when used carefully and with full explanation, can be hugely helpful in depressive disorders in young people and the benefits far outweigh the drawbacks.

Hospitalisation

Inpatient treatment is sometimes needed if there is a serious risk of suicide, such that it is no longer possible to keep your young person safe at home, or if the depression is so profound that it is impacting on the young person's physical health, causing them to be unable to eat or drink or to get out of bed. It may also be recommended if the depression has psychotic features (i.e., where the young person's thinking has lost contact with reality or where he or she may have fixed beliefs that are not true, that they have done something seriously wrong or that people are plotting against them or harming them in some way). Other experiences that may occur in psychotic depression include hearing voices that taunt, threaten or belittle the person. Experiences such as these are extremely frightening for all involved but particularly for the young person. Inpatient treatment may also be suggested where the depression has not responded to outpatient management and more intensive treatment is needed.

Young people who need inpatient care should be treated in an adolescent psychiatry unit, where the ward and daily programme is geared toward young people. Such a unit will have a programme of activities, group meetings and therapy sessions, all aimed at helping young people and their families overcome their difficulties. Inpatient treatment can vary in length from a few days in an acute crisis, to several weeks for more difficult cases. Most units nowadays try to ensure that inpatient treatment is as short as possible and that treatment continues on an outpatient basis when the young person is discharged, because it is in 'the real world' of home, family, school or work that the young person is going to make most progress.

Where resources are inadequate, it may be necessary for your young person to be admitted to an adult psychiatry ward. This is a frightening prospect, which will only be recommended where there is no alternative and where it is essential that your young person is kept safe. Staff in these units are very aware of the risks to young people of being exposed to disturbed adult patients and will take particular care to ensure that their stay is as short as possible.

It can feel as if it is the 'end of the line' if the decision is reached that your young person needs inpatient care, but this is not the case. Many young people who have received inpatient psychiatric treatment make a full recovery and get their lives back on track. Your job as a parent is to give them as much support as you can through this most difficult time, to keep yourself as strong and positive as you can and to keep hope alive.

Day treatment programmes

If you are lucky enough to live near a unit that offers a day treatment programme, this can provide the benefits of intensive treatment without the need for admission to an inpatient unit. Usually, the young person will attend for several hours each day, for individual and group therapy, perhaps for supervision of medication and for therapeutic activities aimed at increasing their confidence. Some of these units have educational facilities that can help greatly to overcome the fears generated by falling behind in schoolwork.

Most adolescent day treatment programmes work in close association with parents or those caring for the young person, and the fact that the young person is living at home while attending the day treatment programme allows a good working relationship to develop between the family and the day programme staff.

Tom's story

(continued from p. 57)

Tom attends the local Child and Adolescent Mental Health Service (CAMHS) unit with his parents. All three are very nervous, not knowing what to expect. They are puzzled by some of the questions they are asked by the two professionals they meet for their first appointment. They are seen together first, then one of the professionals talks to Tom on his own, while the other talks to his parents. Their first visit takes almost 2 hours, but they leave feeling reassured that they understand Tom's situation a bit better and that there is a plan in place to help him. His parents are surprised to be told that Tom has depression, but feel they understand it a bit better when they realise that Tom has had to cope with a lot of upset in the past few years – there has been a good deal of stress in the family as his parents have been having their own difficulties as a couple and have been considering separating, and Tom has not been able to integrate into the secondary school to which he moved last year – he feels bullied and excluded there.

Tom and his parents are told that the plan for treating his depression will involve therapy for Tom and regular meetings with his parents to help them to support Tom's recovery. They are also advised that Tom would benefit from treatment with antidepressant medication (see p. 69). Tom is agreeable to this, as he feels so bad he is willing to try anything to help. His parents are taken aback and have a number of concerns: will he become dependent on the medication, will it change his personality, how long will he have to take it for? They discuss their concerns with the psychiatrist and are given some written information about the medication. They are advised not to make a decision at that point, but to talk it over between themselves and let the psychiatrist know their decision at the next meeting.

Tom's parents decide to ask their family doctor what she thinks. Having met Tom and observed how low his mood was, the doctor advises Tom's parents to go ahead with the medication, which he starts after the next visit to his psychiatrist.

Tom agrees to attend a therapist for help with the problems he had identified (feeling awful, tired, unable to sleep, no friends). Working with the therapist, Tom is helped come up with concrete ways of managing these problems. He attends weekly sessions for the first month and then at 2-weekly intervals for a further 3 months. His parents, who

> *had not been aware of how distressed Tom was at their arguing, decide that they will get some help for themselves as a couple, to help them decide whether to work on improving their own relationship or whether to separate. They meet with Tom's therapist once a month to support the work Tom is doing in therapy, and the therapist gives them some ideas that help with Tom's behaviour at home.*
>
> (continued on p. 94)

How long does it take?

This depends on many factors, some predictable, some less so. Mild to moderate depressive disorders usually respond to treatment over a few weeks to months. Severe depressive disorders can take longer, particularly where they are complicated by social isolation, lack of school attendance and severe family conflict. Studies that have followed up adolescents diagnosed with depressive disorders have shown that almost 80% of them have recovered at 2-year follow-up (see Chapter 11). There is much you can do to support your child and yourself during this time (see Chapter 7).

7

What can parents do?

It is easy to feel overwhelmed when living with someone who is depressed – to almost 'catch' their depression and to feel that nothing can be done to change the situation. But parents can do a lot to help their young person and to help themselves through their child's depression. In fact, parents are vital to helping young people recover and get back on track after a period of depression. In this chapter we consider the things you can do as a parent to help your son or daughter. We also emphasise how important it is not to forget your own needs (or those of other family members) during this difficult time and that you take steps to care for yourself as well.

Supporting your teenager

Recognising when things are not right

When depression shows itself in irritable, angry, moody behaviour (which often seems to be directed mainly at parents), it is common to find yourself reacting in a similar manner, leading to an increasing gulf between you and your teenager. It can be very useful to stand back from the situation and to wonder what might be going on for your son or daughter. How are they feeling? What is going well or badly in their life? What is fuelling their anger? While young people may not respond well to direct questions about such areas – the usual response might be that everything is 'fine' or a rude rebuff advising parents to 'get off my case' – it is important to try and adopt an understanding approach and to help your teenager open up to you. Talking to someone (usually a parent) is the single biggest thing that young people report as being helpful to them in overcoming depression (see Chapter 10). In the following subsections we describe ways to open the lines of communication between you and your teenager.

Keeping a connection

Many parents have found that, while they cannot discuss conflict areas with their young person, they can keep a connection through 'neutral' topics (e.g., TV soaps, football, fashion, etc.) in which they both share an interest. These 'nuggets' of good communication can be fostered and enjoyed for what they are, without trying to slip into 'deeper areas' of conversation. Maintaining a connection with a depressed teenager is especially important. This nurtures your relationship and provides a 'lifeline' between you and your teenager. Teenagers are much more likely to open up to you or seek your help when they are troubled if they already have built up a connection with you. However, it is not necessarily easy to establish a connection with a teenager. They can easily shrug off your attempts to 'get to know them' and you can feel rejected. However, it is worth gently persisting. It may mean that you have to go out of your way to take an interest in your teenager's music rather than criticising it, or learning the details of their favourite soap on the TV rather than dismissing it, or making an effort to share their interest in football rather than saying you don't have the time. These everyday connections form the basis of a good parent–child relationship.

Setting aside time

If your teenager is depressed it is a good idea to make a decision to try and spend some quality (i.e., enjoyable and relaxed) time with them. This is often harder than it can initially seem. Teenagers are caught up in their own lives and depressed teenagers may want to be alone, or certainly not with their parents. However, it is worth persisting and thinking of ways you can spend one-on-one time with your teenager. Though planned activities such as going to a football match or on a shopping trip can work well, often it is informal time together that is the most valuable. You might find a good time is when your teenager comes in from school and is ready to chat, or late at night when they are about to go to bed. When we have asked parents 'what is the best time to chat with their teenager?', one of the most common answer is 'when driving in the car together'. As well as enjoyable chit-chat about ordinary things, conversation about important subjects often comes up when driving with a teenager. This is something to bear in mind when you feel your teenager is treating you like a chauffeur. Use the time to your advantage as an opportunity to spend time with them and to get to know what is going on in their lives.

Active listening

This type of listening has been shown to increase communication and to help young people feel they have been
understood. It involves giving time to young people when
they feel like talking – not easy in our busily scheduled
world. It also involves not interrupting or giving advice,
but commenting on what they are saying in a way that
implies interest and an attempt to understand (e.g., 'that
must have been difficult,' 'I can imagine that must have
been hurtful'). It involves listening to what young people
have to say, without trying to cheer them up or to talk
them out of their feelings.

It can be very upsetting to hear your children speak of
their suffering or their hopelessness, and there is an
understandable tendency to disagree with them, to point
out the good things about their lives, or to try to reassure
them. This can make them feel that you have not
really understood what they are saying and may make it
less likely that they will confide in you again. 'Active
listening' helps them to feel that you are really trying to
understand what they are saying and encourages further
communication.

Parents often wonder about how much to listen to
their teenager's upsets and genuinely worry that this
will cause their teenager to become more stuck in
negative thoughts. The truth is that what is called for is
balance. Teenagers not only need parents who listen
and accept their worries but also parents who will be
reassuring and help them cheer up from time to time.
One mother and teenager girl we worked with used to
get embroiled in long conversations about worries and
negative thoughts, so much so that this was almost the
only conversation that they would have together, leaving
both of them upset and depressed. During family therapy
they changed this pattern: instead of discussing worries all

day long, they restricted it to one conversation a day (just after dinner). At other times both of them tried to talk about other, more positive things in their lives. This balanced approach made a big difference.

Encouraging small steps in a positive direction

Although teenagers can appear not to care, they need lots of encouragement from their parents. Simple compliments, or noticing positive things they do or say, can make a big difference to young people. It is important that this encouragement be given in a genuine way, as teenagers will be the first to shrug off any attention they consider to be 'phoney' or manipulative. Generally, encouragement works best with teenagers if it is matter of fact rather than 'over the top' and if it is specific and clear (whereby you clearly name what you are pleased about and how you feel about it). Remember, each teenager is different; what gets through with one teenager will not work for another. What is important is that you find a way of providing encouragement to your teenager about routine, everyday activities. Giving compliments to teenagers in a genuine way that gets through to them can make a difference:

- noticing when your teenager tries harder at school-work;
- casually thanking your teenager when he does a chore rather than taking it for granted;
- complimenting teenagers on their appearance or what they're wearing.

Encouragement is especially useful for young people who have been depressed. It is important to notice and comment on any small signs of progress. This is the best way to help them get back on track. This can be as simple as noticing and commenting when they are on time for the school bus, or choose to have a shower, or when they clean up the kitchen, or when they don't get drawn into a fight with a brother or sister. A positive comment, while often apparently disregarded by the young person, can help to boost self-esteem and will make it more likely that these small steps of progress will be repeated.

Case history

Mark, who is now 14, was 6 when his parents separated. He lives with his mother and her new husband, his stepfather. His parents have taken active steps to ensure that Mark can have a good relationship with both of them. He used to spend most weekends with his father, until his father met a new partner two years ago. Mark does not get on too well with his father's partner, and when she and his father had a baby daughter he found this very hard to cope with. He no longer wants to spend weekends with his father, which disrupts both families. There is increasing conflict between Mark and all four parental figures in his life and between Mark's mother and father, who each feel that the other is responsible for Mark's difficulties.

Mark becomes increasingly irritable and withdrawn. He goes in late for school, does little work and stays in his room most weekends. After a row with his mother, he takes an overdose of paracetamol and is admitted to a children's hospital. During his assessment there he speaks of how he always hoped his mother and father would get back together, but when his Dad's new baby arrived he realised this would not happen. He feels that his father now has no time for him when he visits and feels that no one understands his hurt and upset.

The overdose is a wake-up call for Mark's parents who realise the seriousness of what is going on. As a result they make a decision to do things differently. They try to put aside their own disagreements and to focus on Mark's needs. Despite his new family, the father tries to be more available for Mark when he visits, arranging activities they could do together such as going to football. This initially doesn't run smoothly as Mark shrugs off his father's attempts to spend time with him, often arranging to do other things or refusing to go out at all. His father persists though and discovers that, rather than arranging an outing, the best thing was to be around at informal times for Mark. He discovers that Mark is open for chatting late at night just before bedtime or when they are driving somewhere together. The father makes the most of these connections. In addition, the father takes an interest in Mark's favourite soap on TV. This becomes a regular conversation point between them as they joke about the lives of the soap characters. Over time, Mark begins to open up a little to his father and their relationship improves. On one occasion Mark breaks down and speaks of the struggles he has making friends in school and his father is able to support him. His father later thinks to himself how pleased he is that Mark confided in him when he was upset, rather than taking an overdose like he did before.

Dealing with discipline and conflict

In normal situations parenting a teenager can be daunting and challenging. Teenagers are at a time of life when they are separating from parents and learning how to be their own person. This inevitably leads to conflict, as teenagers push against rules and limits as they seek independence. Yet teenagers need the support and guidance of their parents more than ever. The challenge of being a parent of a teenager is to be both firm as you negotiate rules and boundaries as well as supportive and encouraging as you stay involved and connected in their lives. The long-term aim is to help teenagers grow up and take responsibility for their own lives, as well as helping them form good relationships with other people.

Parenting a depressed teenager is particularly challenging. Because of the depression you might feel confused as how best to respond. You might wonder to what extent you should ask your teenager to do normal things and how much to allow for their depression. Often you can feel you are 'walking on eggshells', scared of pushing them too far. The truth of the matter is that, like normal teenagers, young people who are depressed need a balanced, flexible approach from their parents. They need parents who will be there to support and encourage them, but who are also not afraid to be firm and to challenge them to take responsibility. In the following four subsections we briefly describe four principles for resolving conflict and managing discipline with teenagers:

1 pressing the pause button;

2 actively listening;

3 assertively giving your point of view; and

4 negotiating and giving choices.

Pressing the pause button

When a young person is rude and abusive, breaks rules or
is 'difficult', it is easy to get sucked into a full-scale row,
with shouting, saying things you regret later or even
physical violence. In such situations 'pressing the pause
button' can help you as a parent to stay in control, to
decide how you want to handle the situation and to
avoid saying or doing things that may damage your relationship with your child. 'Pressing the pause button'
involves taking a deep breath, keeping one's temper,
often withdrawing from the situation, while explaining
that you are too angry/upset to deal with it now, but you
will later.

Case history

*John, aged 14, was told to be home from the disco by
midnight. Peter, his father, waited up, but John did
not arrive. He tried to call him on his mobile, but
John had switched it off. Peter became more and
more anxious and angry when John still did not
come home. At 2 a.m. John arrived home, smelling
strongly of alcohol. Peter's instinctive reaction was
to ' have a go', to tell John just what he thought of
him and what the consequences of his behaviour
would be. Instead, recognising that neither John
nor himself were in the best frame of mind for
dealing with the situation, he opened the door, told*

> *John he was very annoyed by what had happened,*
> *did not respond to John's excuses and said he would*
> *discuss it with him in the morning.*
>
> *The following day, Peter spoke to John about*
> *what had happened. He listened, without arguing*
> *back, as John explained that all his friends had*
> *been drinking and were allowed out until 2 a.m.*
> *Peter made it clear that, because of what happened,*
> *John would not be allowed to attend the next disco in*
> *3 weeks' time and would have to be in 1 hour earlier*
> *for the following week. Peter remained in control*
> *and was not drawn into an argument with John,*
> *who reluctantly accepted the consequences of his*
> *behaviour.*

Actively listening

Active listening means setting time aside to understand and appreciate your young person's point of view. It means going out of your way to place yourself in their shoes and to understand where they are coming from. Rather than seeing their depression as something trivial, it means understanding more deeply how things are difficult for them and the struggles they are going through. Rather than reacting to their irritable mood, active listening means working hard to understand what is at the bottom of it (e.g., perhaps they have had a bad day at school).

Active listening is particularly important in discipline issues. Rather than immediately confronting your teenager over staying out late, or the untidy room, or poor school performance, it is worth trying to listen first to understand their point of view. This approach is more likely to be successful. In practical terms, active listening involves setting time aside to talk problems through with your young person. Generally, it means 'pressing the pause button' and not immediately reacting, but instead taking time to acknowledge and understand things from your teenager's perspective.

Assertively giving your point of view

As well as being a good listener, good parenting involves being able to assertively challenge and respectfully confront young people. Good parents don't turn a blind eye to their son's drinking or his increasing withdrawal or moodiness, or avoid talking about their daughter's increasing poor school performance. As well as listening, good parenting is about being able to assertively give your own point of view. *Being able to both listen and assertively give your point of view is the basis of resolving most conflicts.* Of course it does matter how you go about giving your point of view. If you are overbearing, blaming or too angry, teenagers are not likely to listen. Equally, it is important not to be passive, where you don't get your view across for fear of upsetting your teenager, or you back down too easily and let your teenager walk all over you. Rather, the aim is to speak up assertively, whereby you communicate respectfully and calmly what you feel and think, making sure to express your positive intentions and feelings. For example, rather than saying 'what the hell do you mean staying out late like that, you had me worried sick?', it might be more effective to say 'I worry about you being out late, especially when it is dark. You see I need to know you are safe.'

Negotiating and giving choices

The secret to discipline with teenagers is negotiation. Rather than simply imposing rules, it is important to discuss rules and limits with teenagers and where possible to negotiate compromises. This process of negotiation not only helps you arrive at the best solutions and ones your teenager might keep, it also teaches teenagers how to communicate and helps maintain a connection between parent and teenager.

Giving young people choices and consequences helps teach them responsibility. Rather than get into an argument with your depressed young person when you want them to do something they don't want to do – it can be helpful to give choices instead. For example, the depressed young person who cannot face school and wants to say home all day while you are at work can be given the choice of either going to school or going to his aunt for the day. Or the depressed young person who is spending hours in his bedroom, with curtains drawn and dishes and rubbish accumulating, can be given the choice of cleaning and airing the bedroom himself or you will do it on health grounds. It is important that only choices that can be enforced are given and to make them as simple and clear-cut as possible. Depressed young people often have great difficulty with decision making, so when they do make a choice this is an opportunity for you to praise a small step in a positive direction.

Case history

The parents of Sheila, 14, had become increasingly worried about her moodiness and withdrawal. She was spending more and more time in her room, avoided going out and seemed to be losing contact with friends. Her school performance was beginning to suffer. Sheila's parents had given up nagging her to come out of her room or to get up on time for school as it didn't seem to make a difference. Sheila would either fly off the handle or ignore them completely. Concerned, the parents consulted with a psychologist at Sheila's school who suggested to them that Sheila might be depressed.

Together they discussed the different strategies that could be used to help Sheila. First, they decided that one of them should have a chat with Sheila. They agreed that the mother might have the best chance of getting through to Sheila, and she chose to have a conversation with Sheila after dinner as this was a time when she was up and about and at her most positive. When they spoke the mother adopted a calm, concerned but firm manner with Sheila. She explained how concerned she and Sheila's father were about her and that they could not let her continue to miss school and to stay all day in her room like she was. Sheila initially got angry saying she 'just wanted to be left alone'. Her mother remained calm and said she understood Sheila wanted to be left alone, but that she as her mother could not stand by and do nothing. Sheila walked away from the conversation. The mother remained calm and waited to approach Sheila later, saying 'listen Sheila we have to talk ...'. Sheila at this point opened up a little and spoke of how lonely and low she was. This was a little bit of a break-through and her mother listened carefully.

> *Later they began to negotiate about what they could do to sort the problem out. They agreed that Sheila could not spend all evening in her room and that she had to come down for her dinner at the table and/or go out once a day. They began to talk about how to help her get back into a school routine and sought the help of the school psychologist. This new respectful but firm and persistent approach by the parents signalled a change and over time things began to improve for Sheila.*

Keeping yourself going

Looking after yourself

This might involve making sure you eat properly, get some exercise and have regular 'outside of the family' time. This includes pursuing a hobby or interest you have, or spending time with a friend who knows something of your situation. It is easy to feel that you cannot leave your depressed child in case something happens, but you do need to 'recharge your batteries'. You will come back to the family refreshed and with renewed energy. If you have serious concerns about something happening when you are out – perhaps the other parent or a friend can hold the fort while you are gone.

If you are under a great deal of stress yourself, such that you are depressed, drinking too much or angry all the time, it is well worth seeking your own help, separate from that which your child may be receiving. Helping yourself in this way may be the first step on the road to helping your child.

Strength in numbers

Some parents find it helpful to join a support group for families with a depressed family member. They feel really understood when they meet other people who know what it is like to live with a depressed young person and often pick up useful ideas that can help their own situation. It may be useful to make contact with local services to seek out these supports in your area.

Helping your other children to cope

The demands of caring for a young person with depression can put great strain on the whole family. Other children may feel that they are being overlooked, while the troubled and troublesome child gets all the attention. This may sow seeds of resentment that are neither helpful to the recovery of the depressed young person nor to your other children.

Explanation

It is helpful to explain to your other children your view of your depressed child's difficulties. Children (and indeed many adults) do not understand terms like 'depression'. It may be more useful to say: 'Sinead is going through a very difficult time just now. I know it is frustrating and upsetting for everyone, but we need to try to be patient with her. She will get over it, but it is going to take quite a while. We need to try to help her and each other.'

It is perfectly normal for the other children to be very angry with the depressed child, and it is helpful for them to be able to express their anger without feeling blamed or responsible for the depressed child's problems. Giving time to the other children helps, as does active listening and positive attention. It may help the other children in the family to understand and cope better with the situation if they are included in the family work which may be part of your child's treatment.

Keeping family activities going

Life can seem to grind to a halt when a family member has depression. So, the activities and interests of the other children should be fostered, if this can be arranged. Family celebrations, holidays, etc. should not stop, just because the depressed young person does not want to take part. To enable this to happen means you need to get as much support as you can from family members. Don't be afraid to tell your extended family – most people try to understand and will be helpful if asked to do specific things (e.g., collect a child from football for you, take your child out with their family for the day). Grandparents can be very supportive, if they are called on.

Tackling family problems

All families have problems. The difference between healthy and unhealthy families is how they deal with them. Healthy families acknowledge that problems exist, try to discuss them together and take steps to try and solve them. Young people with depression sometimes come from families where problems are denied, cannot be spoken about and so cannot be solved. Some family problems cannot be solved, but acknowledging that the problem is there and trying to sort it out can be very helpful to a young person.

Conflicting advice from family members/friends

Many parents find this one of the most difficult things to cope with. Everyone will have a different view on 'what you should do', while you know all the things you have tried without success to do. This advice is sometimes so annoying that parents cut themselves off from family and friends, becoming increasingly isolated themselves.

It helps to keep in mind that the advice is being given to try to help you. However, it does not feel helpful. This could be similar to how a depressed young person feels when people try to 'talk him out' of his depression. Maybe it makes his responses to such talking a bit easier to understand!

Perhaps you could explain to your extended family and friends that you understand their wish to help, but you want a break from talking about problems and what would be really helpful would be a cup of coffee and a chat about anything else, or a companion to go walking with, or a babysitter! Most people respond when asked and feel good that they are being really helpful.

What parents can't do

You cannot *make* your young person get over their depression or be happy. Much as you may wish you could, you can't. You can however support them through it and keep hope alive.

You cannot make friends for your young person. Many adolescents with depression are isolated and lonely and parents long for them to have friends, which they feel would solve many of their problems. You can support any small attempt by your young person toward making friends, even if it only involves answering the phone or going into a shop on her own. These are small steps toward reduced social isolation and are pointers toward things getting better.

Tom's story

(continued from p. 75)

As well as attending psychotherapy at the adolescent mental health service, Tom's parents also try to make changes at home to help his progress. Both his parents make an effort to make time available to chat with him. His mother fosters a connection with him about one of the TV soaps. His parents also make a special effort to be particularly encouraging toward Tom, noticing any small steps of progress: when he watches a TV programme with the family, they comment on how good it is to have him there; when he avoids getting into a row with his younger sister, they comment on the restraint he

---

has shown. Both parents work hard not to respond with anger when he is angry, and the atmosphere at home becomes calmer.

Tom decides to start football training again, which they quietly encourage without putting him under pressure. His father is available to drive him to and from the training and uses this opportunity to chat with Tom about football and other neutral topics. Tom is still not back at school full time, being late on several days of the week when he cannot or does not get up on time. His parents notice the days he does get up on time and encourage this.

Tom's parents have discussed his difficulties with the school principal and together they have come up with a plan to help him. The teachers accept his being late, but insist that he covers the work that was done in the classes he missed. They are encouraging of Tom's efforts, but are clear in their expectations of him.

Tom improves gradually, and over the next 6 months his 'old self' starts to re-emerge. He now trains regularly for football and occasionally goes out with some of the team after a training session. He is back at school full time and is sleeping better. He can still be 'snappy' at home at times, but this is nothing like it was before. He can be heard singing and whistling in the bathroom and has to be told to keep his music down.

Tom feels he no longer needs the antidepressant medication, but he is advised to continue taking it for at least a further 6 months. He will then have been taking it for one year. The plan is to then reduce it gradually over a further 3 months, with a view to stopping it.

His parents are delighted with the changes they see in Tom. They are still uncertain about their own future together, but feel that, with all they have been through, they will be able to help Tom cope with whatever decision they make for themselves.

8

Suicide and self-harm

Suicide rates have risen sharply in most Westernised cultures in the past 10–15 years, particularly in young adult males. In Ireland suicide is now a leading cause of death in 15–24-year-old males, while in the UK and USA it is the second most common cause of death in males in this age group. Sadly, there are few families in Ireland who have not had experience of the death by suicide of some young person, either a relative or friend of a family member. While some deaths by suicide do appear to happen genuinely 'out of the blue', we know that in many cases people close to the young person have been aware that things have not been all right for them for some time and have had concerns about them. Some of these young people have had depressive disorders that often have not been diagnosed or treated.

Suicide is a major concern of parents of young people with depression. Though often not discussed, the concern is usually in the back of most parents' minds, and they often fear that mentioning it may in some way make it more likely to happen.

Some myths about suicide

There is a myth that people who speak about dying by suicide rarely commit suicide. This is not true. Young people who talk about committing suicide should always be taken seriously. Research has shown that about 25% of people who die from suicide have told someone in the few months preceding their death that they are suicidal.

Another myth is that asking someone whether he is suicidal may 'tip him over the edge'. This also is not true. It can be a great relief to someone who is struggling with suicidal thoughts to be able to voice their concerns to someone who understands and can offer support.

A further myth is that once someone has been suicidal he or she will always be suicidal. This is not the case. People with depression can sometimes see no way forward and see suicide as the only way to end their pain. When their depression has lifted, these suicidal thoughts usually disappear.

Are there warning signs?

There are common warning signs of depression but much fewer warning signs of suicide – the act itself is thankfully still rare. The warning signs of depression are outlined in Chapter 2 – changes in mood, loss of previous interest in school, job, hobbies, sports, friends, marked irritability, changes in sleep pattern, etc. These are common signs that indicate the young person has some difficulties and are worth looking into further. They are not warning signs of suicide.

There are a few warning signs that a young person may be suicidal. Those who have made suicide attempts in the past are more at risk than those who have not. The death by suicide of someone close to the young person, or admired by them, increases the risk. Talking of suicide, being preoccupied with death, giving away possessions, saying goodbye to family and friends all may indicate that the young person is actively suicidal.

What to do if you suspect your young person is suicidal

Do not be afraid to talk to him, to ask him if he is OK, if he is feeling down or if life does not seem worth living. Try to listen to him and not to talk him out of how he says he is feeling, and it is best not to try to cheer him up. If he does admit to having suicidal thoughts, try to find out how well developed these are: Had he thought what he would do or how to do it? Fleeting thoughts of suicide are common in adolescents, but having a well-thought-out plan or being preoccupied with death or suicide is not common.

If your young person is actively suicidal, it is important to try to get a mental health service for him. This may involve going to your local hospital A&E department as the most direct route in a crisis. In other situations, when you have to wait to see a doctor or psychiatrist, it is important to take practical steps to ensure your child's safety. This can include making sure someone supportive is with them at all times and removing tablets or other dangerous items from the household.

Coping with suicide attempts

Fortunately, actual suicide is still relatively rare, though suicide attempts happen much more frequently. Both boys and girls attempt suicide, and this is an obvious indication that all is not well for the young person. Suicide attempts often occur after a conflict or stress, such as a row with a parent or friend, a break-up with boyfriend/girlfriend or other stressful event, but these events do not *cause* suicide attempts. Most young people who row with parents or break up with friends do not attempt suicide. Young people who do attempt suicide after such events are particularly vulnerable because of some other ongoing difficulties. For this reason it is important to get help for a young person who has attempted suicide. The direct route to help is through a hospital's A&E department, where your child's medical needs will be attended to and a mental health professional will ascertain what further help is needed.

Most parents are devastated when their child attempts suicide. It is normal to feel angry and deeply hurt as well as very scared about what might have happened. It is easy to swing between feeling angry at yourself for neither noticing the signs nor being there for your child and feeling angry at your child for doing such a 'stupid' and devastating thing. Once the initial shock has worn off parents can react by either 'putting the event in the back of their mind', trying not to talk about it again or by becoming hypervigilant constantly watching their child. Generally, we recommend a 'middle response' as the best way to help in these situations, which includes:

1 A frank and honest conversation between parent and child (sometimes assisted by a professional) about

the circumstances that led up to the suicide attempt. It is important that you take time to appreciate your child's feelings as well as communicating to them how you feel.

2 Devising a plan to address the problems that led up to the suicide attempt, such as addressing the stressful situations that affect your child.

3 A plan to improve family communication and relationships, which should include efforts to build on good times and enjoyable events.

4 A realistic plan to manage discipline problems in the future (see the next section).

Though a suicide attempt is a devastating event in a family, we try and invite parents and young people to see it as a 'turning point' or as an opportunity for change. It is fortunate that your child was not successful. You now have an opportunity to move on and address the problems that were happening and to work hard at making improvements in your family life.

Dealing with discipline after a suicide attempt

After a suicide attempt it can be challenging for parents to manage discipline. The next time you attempt to enforce a rule ('No, you cannot stay the night with your friend'), you will worry that your young person may do 'something stupid' and attempt suicide again. This can lead to a 'walking on eggshells' atmosphere at home and the consequence of not having healthy and necessary discipline in place.

It is important, however, not to back off from discipline, but to continue to negotiate with your child, agreeing clear rules and consequences. If the suicide attempt happened after a row or disagreement it helps to have a discussion with your child about this. You want to let them know that you understand their distress, but you do not see suicidal behaviour as ever right or justified. Your aim is to help them find other healthier ways in which they might manage their upset and anger next time there is a row or disagreement. Just as in normal circumstances, teenagers who have attempted suicide need not only parents who are both encouraging and supportive but also parents who are not afraid to set boundaries and to be calm and firm regarding discipline. The aim is to help your teenager take responsibility for their actions.

Case history

Tanya, aged 14, took an overdose of paracetamol after a row with her mother. She had wanted to go to a disco with her friends, but her parents felt she was too young. She became frightened after taking the tablets and told her sister, who then told her mother. Tanya was brought to hospital immediately, where she was given medication to make her vomit the tablets, and she was kept in for overnight observation.

The next day Tanya met with a social worker from the mental health team who talked with her about what had happened. The social worker also met her parents, who spoke of how difficult Tanya had been over the past few months, staying out late, mixing with friends her parents did not approve of and truanting from school. Tanya said she was fed up with all the rows and had just wanted to get away from everything. She regretted taking the overdose and was fearful that it would lead to even more rows at home.

The social worker suggested to Tanya and her parents that it would be a good idea to plan some further sessions after Tanya's discharge, to help with communication in the family. Tanya was not too keen, but agreed reluctantly. Her parents were relieved to be able to talk over their worries about how to handle things the next time they had to say 'no' to their daughter.

Tanya was discharged from hospital after 2 days. Her parents had been able, while she was in hospital, to spend some time deciding how best to handle her homecoming. They decided, despite their fear and anger, that they would try to understand how difficult coping with adolescence was for Tanya and would make an effort to communicate with her, using some of the ideas the social worker had discussed with them. They were compassionate and made it clear to Tanya that her safety was most important to them and, while they would try to reach a compromise in many situations, there would be times when they would have to say 'no' to her demands.

Three weeks later Tanya wanted to go with her friends to a concert to hear her favourite group playing. Her parents had misgivings because of what they had heard could happen at events such as this. Because they were now able to talk to Tanya and had said to her how pleased they were that she had been making an effort to come in on time, they agreed she could attend the concert provided they collected her after it. Tanya said this would be very embarrassing for her in front of her friends. Her parents gave her the choice of going and being collected, or not going at all. She chose to go and was collected along with two of her friends, giving Tanya's parents a chance to meet her friends.

Dealing with self-cutting behaviour

I think it was just because the pain built up so badly that I used to cut myself. When my friends asked me why I did it, I used to say 'if you put a potato in the microwave and you take it out, it's steaming, you cut it to release some of the steam' – so that's what I used to do. Seeing myself bleed made me feel a bit like I was punishing myself or something and it made me feel better.

Ella, aged 15

Sometimes young people who are very angry or upset cut themselves as a way of relieving tension. They commonly cut their wrists or forearms, using a knife, razor blade, broken glass or some other sharp implement. They explain that the pain they experience when they cut themselves is preferable to the emotional pain that leads up to the cutting and that it helps to relieve their emotional pain. This may be very hard for us as adults to understand, and parents are often deeply upset and angered by this behaviour. It helps me, as a therapist, to understand this a little better when I remember that many people when they are very angry or upset also use techniques that involve hurting themselves as a way of coping (e.g., pinching themselves, biting the inside of their cheeks, banging their fists against the wall). Self-harming behaviour is often a habit that has built up over time that the teenager uses as a means of managing distress and coping with feelings.

Not all young people who cut themselves are depressed, and only some of them are suicidal, but they are troubled and do need help. Parents who notice marks or cuts on their teenagers arms should ask how they got them and not be fobbed off by such replies as 'I was only messing about' or 'everyone does it'. It is a good idea to try and get your teenager to talk about it and to seek help if necessary. The aim of treatment is, first, to get the teenager to open up and talk about the behaviour (as often it can be a big secret) and the feelings that underlie it. Then, the focus becomes helping the teenager identify other more helpful ways of dealing with these feelings (such as talking when upset, or trying to change negative thoughts, or distracting oneself with other activities). Over time the aim is to help the young person break the habit of self-harming behaviour and develop healthy ways of addressing his or her troubles.

Suicide and alcohol

Alcohol itself does not cause suicide, but vulnerable young people who drink to excess are at greater risk of

suicide than those who don't. About a quarter of young
people who commit suicide have excessive amounts of
alcohol in their blood stream. There is evidence to show
that alcohol may act on the brain to reduce the normal
inhibitory nerve pathways that keep impulsive and self-
damaging behaviour in check.

Many young people in our culture binge-drink regularly to get drunk, sometimes profoundly so. This pattern
of drinking in a young person with depression is worrying
and self-harming, as excessive alcohol tends to make
depression worse. If your young person with depression
is drinking in this way, it is worth putting energy into
getting help for him.

Excessive drinking can lead to depression, and it can
be difficult to know which came first – depression or
drinking. It is easy for a young person (who is depressed
as a result of excessive drinking) to get into a vicious circle
of drinking leading to depression leading to further
drinking in an attempt to ease the pain of depression
(see Chapter 4 for more information on alcohol problems).

9

Dealing with common problems

Depressive disorders in young people show themselves in different ways, but tend to affect all areas of their lives to some degree. This chapter deals with some common problems that can emerge when parenting a young person who is depressed.

Depression and school

Depressed young people often find school very difficult and are reluctant to attend. They often suffer anxiety that stems from their depression, manifesting itself in physical symptoms on school mornings that ease off as the day progresses. These symptoms may include nausea, stomach pains, fatigue and weakness. If they do go to school and make a start on the school day, the symptoms tend to ease off. These are not 'put on' or imagined, they are real symptoms of anxiety. Other

children may become panic-stricken at the idea of attending school, with a fear that they cannot explain.

While some depressed young people will need some
time off school, the aim should be to get them back to
school as soon as possible. Starting back for half-days
may make things easier, although this does not appeal to
some adolescents who have a dread of being 'different'
from others in their class. They may need firm encouragement to attend and may need a parent to accompany them
for a while. Long periods out of school can cause further
problems, as fears grow that they will not be able to catch
up on what they have missed and as they become more cut
off from their classmates.

Other depressed young people attend school, but their
school work deteriorates due to problems with concentration and self-organisation. Those who are perfectionists
may spend increasing hours at their homework, never
satisfied that they have done enough or have got it right.
Others may lose interest in their work and appear not to
care. This may get them into trouble in school, making
school more difficult to attend.

It is a good idea to inform your child's year head or
form tutor about his difficulties. Once informed, most but
not all schools are sympathetic and supportive and will
make allowances for your child's difficulties.

Depression and exams

All would agree that sitting for major public examinations
is stressful, but there is little evidence to support the idea
that those sitting major exams are at any greater risk of
depression or suicidal behaviour than anyone else of their

age. Rates of suicide in young people do not show an increase related to the timing of exams or exam results.

There are however some young people who may have been struggling psychologically for whom a major exam is just one stress too many and who may become depressed as the exam approaches. Those who have low self-esteem, an anxious personality and are very perfectionistic, who always feel their best is not good enough, are most at risk. Often these are young people whose whole sense of worth is built on academic success, who do not have other 'buffers' such as friends, sports or hobbies to provide emotional outlets.

Parents often wonder where the cut-off point is between 'normal' exam stress and depression. Most parents who have helped young people through major exams would agree that moodiness, irritability, strange eating patterns and intense self-absorption fall within the 'normal' range, whereas crippling anxiety, severe sleep disturbance, regular expressions of futility and hopelessness, and any type of self-injurious behaviour does not. Chapter 2 contains some useful information to help parents recognise depressive disorders in young people.

If your child does have a depressive disorder and is due to sit a major public examination, such as the Leaving Certificate in Ireland or GCSEs in the UK, careful consideration should be given to whether they should continue to try to study and sit the exam or whether it might be best to defer it for a year, as they are unlikely to be able to give of their best while suffering from depression. Some depressed young people want to 'get it over with' and wish to sit the exams, and they can be supported to do this. The exam can always be repeated when the young person has recovered. Marie Murray has written an excellent book – *Surviving the Leaving Cert* – for parents of students sitting the Leaving Certificate in

Ireland, but it is relevant to parents of any young person sitting a major 'end of secondary school' examination. Details are given in the Resources section at the end of this book.

He won't go for help

As outlined in Chapter 5, not all young people with depressive disorders need specialised mental health treatment. Those with severe depression whose health is being affected by under or overeating, or have become totally withdrawn and unable to participate in life, or have become cut off from reality and believe they are wholly bad, or are suicidal, do need specialised help.

A number of approaches to persuading your young person to accept help are outlined in Chapter 5. Most young people will eventually accept help, but there are a small number who still refuse. Their refusal is usually due to a mixture of fear and the negative thinking that is part of depression. How best to proceed depends on the severity of the situation. If your child's life is on hold, with him spending all the time locked away in his room, or if you believe he is suicidal or is harming himself, or is out of contact with reality, then a big effort to get him the necessary help is called for. This might involve discussing the situation with your general practitioner, getting a referral to your local mental health services, discussing the situation with them and arranging an appointment. Once this has been done, a united approach involving both parents and perhaps other relatives can be made in which the adults state their concerns to the young person and tell him that an appointment has been made, what it will involve and who will accompany him. It is very difficult for a young person to refuse a calm, united, firm approach of this kind. It is difficult and troublesome to set this up, but is well worth doing.

If this does not work, discuss the situation with your local mental health service. They may have a community psychiatric nurse as part of their mental health team who might be prepared to make a home visit and who will be skilled in communicating with reluctant people.

Involuntary admission to a psychiatric hospital is reserved for those whose mental illness is causing a danger to their own lives or the lives of other people. It is very occasionally necessary to use it to prevent death or serious harm befalling a young person or a family member. The age at which young people can be involuntarily committed to a psychiatric hospital, and the mechanism for doing it, varies from country to country, and it needs to be discussed with your general practitioner and local mental health service.

Sleep problems

These are common in depressed young people who often take several hours to get off to sleep at night or may wake frequently. They are particularly common where there is no routine to the child's day, where they may sleep until early afternoon and then be unable to settle to sleep until four or five the following morning.

You can encourage your child to have a bedtime routine, such as having a warm drink and some supper, a bath or shower and going to bed at the same time as the rest of the family, with a view to reading or listening to relaxing music until he or she falls asleep. Most adolescents will have difficulty sticking to such a routine, but it is worth a try.

Having to get up in the morning for school or work makes it less likely that the young person will slip into the 'awake all night/asleep all day' pattern. But even with such a day-time routine, some young people have serious sleep problems that seem to be part of the depressive disorder. Some antidepressant medications can help also with sleep problems, while some may make sleep problems worse. It is worth discussing this with your child's doctor. Most doctors are understandably reluctant to prescribe sleeping tablets for young people, but where sleep disturbance is very severe a brief 3 or 4-week course may be prescribed to help break a cycle of sleep disturbance leading to anxiety about being able to sleep, leading to further sleep disturbance.

Anger and aggression

Anger and aggression are common in depression in young people and are often the most prominent symptoms. Usually the aggression is verbal and often is in response to the young person being asked to do something they don't want to do. You may find that 'pressing the pause button' (yours) and other approaches outlined in Chapter 7 can help to reduce aggression and anger. Physical aggression that may include damaging furniture, breaking windows or destroying household items should not be acceptable, even if the young person is depressed. Should it happen, the young person should have to repair or replace the items they have destroyed, even though it may take them some time to be able to afford this.

Serious physical violence to family members is rare, but can happen. This is more likely in depressed young people who have had behavioural difficulties for many years before they become depressed. In some extreme situations it may be necessary to call the police and to press charges where physical violence has got out of hand. Being depressed does not justify injuring people.

Depression and bullying

There is a link between depression and bullying. Many young people who have had depressive disorders describe how being bullied was one of the main causes of their depression. Certainly, young people with depression are vulnerable to being bullied, as they are often 'on the edge' of things in school, are somewhat withdrawn and are without close friends.

The types of bullying suffered by older adolescents is often of the more psychological type and may be hard to describe. Being deliberately excluded from activities that 'friends' are planning, being sent cruel or insulting text messages, having untrue stories spread about you, being called a 'psycho' – these are experiences that some young people have to endure on a daily basis:

> *I was really badly bullied. I don't know how I coped really. There were some times when I just couldn't. 'Coz I thought it was my own problem that all these people didn't like me. You get into that mentality and it's constantly with you every day, beating you down until you turn on yourself.*
> Luke, aged 14

If you suspect your child is being bullied, what can you do? You can try to talk to them and support them by finding strategies to deal with the bully. Many older children and teenagers will find it hard to admit they are being bullied, even when they are. This is because of a mixture of shame and guilt, and a fear that bringing the bullying to attention will make things worse. It is important to be sensitive to these feelings and fears.

If you suspect bullying at school, talk to your child's year head. Subtle psychological bullying can be very hard to detect – things like being called names, left out of groups, not included in class outings. Many schools nowadays have an active antibullying policy and have good ideas how to help where bullying is suspected. They are sensitive to the wishes of the bullied young person not to be identified.

10

Learning from young people who have recovered from depression

Carol Fitzpatrick, John Sharry,
Suzanne Guerin and Katherine O'Hanlon

What helps young people to get over depression? We know quite a lot from research studies about factors that increase the risk of a young person developing depression, but we know relatively little about what helps them to get over depression once they already have it. We know that most young people with depressive disorders do recover, but some are at risk of having further episodes during their lifetime (see Chapter 1). We know that some forms of therapy, such as cognitive behavioural therapy (CBT), are effective for depression that is of a mild to moderate level of severity, while antidepressant medication combined with CBT can be effective for more severe forms of depression. This information is available to us from carefully designed research studies. But very little research has been carried out in which young people themselves have been asked their views about what it was like to experience depression, how it affected them and what helped them to recover. This type of research is being carried out increasingly in health services, where consumers' views may be very different from those of the health care professionals.

The *Working Things Out* study

The recently completed *Working Things Out* study was a joint project involving University College Dublin and the Department of Child and Family Psychiatry in the Mater Hospital in Dublin. The study set out to seek the views of young people who had recovered from depression about their experience and what had helped them to recover. The study involved in-depth interviews with two groups of young people. The first group had attended the Department of Child and Family Psychiatry for treatment of depression. The second group had also been through a period of depression, but had not attended mental health services – they were recruited through a large study to identify depressive disorders in young secondary school students. The adolescents were aged 13 to 16 years and all had 'come through' their depression at the time they participated in the interviews for the *Working Things Out* project. The young people all gave informed consent for their participation in the project, as did their parents, and they gave permission for the information they gave to be made available in an anonymous form to other young people, to their parents and to mental health professionals. They knew that the ideas they gave might in the future be used in the development of a treatment programme for adolescents with depression and were keen that this should happen.

The interviews were carried out by a psychology

graduate, Katherine O'Hanlon, who was not part of the treatment team. This made it more likely that the young people would be comfortable enough with her to talk about both the positive and negative aspects of the treatment they had received. Each interview was open-ended, taking as much or as little time as the young people needed to give their views. In practice the shortest interview took 45 minutes, while the longest took 1 hour 45 minutes, the rest falling somewhere between these two extremes. The interviews were audiotaped and were later transcribed and analysed for common themes.

In this project we did not use the terms 'depression' or 'depressive disorder' when talking with the young people, as they rarely labelled their experience in this way. Instead, we referred to 'having been through a difficult time in your life when you were "down" and things seemed very hard'. This was how the young people themselves viewed the time they were experiencing what we would call a 'depressive disorder'.

The interviews were carried out in a way that encouraged the young people to give their views. They were asked how it felt when they were depressed, what they thought had caused them to feel like that and what had helped them to recover.

Twenty-one adolescents took part in the project, 11 boys and 10 girls, with just over half belonging to the group who had attended the department for treatment of depression. The youngest participant was 13 years old and the remainder were 14 to 16 years old. The most striking thing about the project was the enthusiasm shown by the young people involved in it. They seemed to value being asked their views 'as experts' in getting through a difficult period in their lives and gave willingly of their time for no reward other than knowing that the information they were giving might help other young people.

What it felt like when they were depressed

Many of the young people described their experiences of being depressed in great detail. They used words like 'sad', 'lonely', 'confused', 'angry', but only one-third used the word 'depressed'. Some of the descriptions they gave are shown on p. 7 and in the quotations below. The sense of isolation – being cut off from other people or in conflict with them – comes over very strongly, as does the feeling of hopelessness – that nothing could ever be different. Just over one-half of the young people reported that they had considered suicide during the time in question and one-quarter of them had attempted suicide.

Loss of confidence

> *Well, I suppose you just kind of feel sad and you lose confidence in yourself. You're not as talkative with your friends, you don't really enjoy doing anything any more. Things you used to look forward to, they don't really matter any more.*
>
> David, aged 15

Loss of interest

> *I couldn't get up in the mornings. I wasn't really interested in anything. I couldn't be bothered doing anything – stuff like that.*
>
> Luke, aged 14

Easily upset

You get upset really easily. Like even the smallest thing would upset you. Like even a small fight with one of your friends will really upset you.

David, aged 15

Anger

I'd get really angry sometimes and just lash out at people. Even if they hadn't done anything I'd take it out on other people.

Gary, aged 14

Yeah – it's like if I'm in a really bad mood or upset for no reason, I'll snap really easily for no reason at my parents. Like if my mam asked me to do something, I'd snap at her and shout at her. I don't mean to do that but I just do.

Beckie, aged 14

Concentration

I couldn't really concentrate that much. My head was somewhere else. I wouldn't even know what I was thinking about. One second I'd be concentrating and then I'd just wander off in a little world of my own for a while. I started dropping down, my results just started dropping. The teachers were on at me 'cos I wouldn't hand up projects on time – things like that.

Shellie, aged 15

*After my granddad died I just stopped doing work
in school. Like I didn't do any study or anything. I
just couldn't be bothered to do any. I just didn't see
the point of it.*

Martin, aged 15

Risk taking

*I had no aversion to death if it just happened. I'd
take stupid risks and preservation of life would not
be a priority.*

David, aged 16

Suicidal thoughts

*You just think 'it's going to be better when I'm
gone.' Like, 'my family's going to be OK' and
'school's going to be so much better for everyone
else when I'm gone.' So it's like you're doing it
for everyone else as well, plus you hate yourself so
much.*

Sean, aged 15

*I used to think about suicide a lot, and then when
my parents found out how I was feeling, that was
the first thing that crossed their minds, but I think
it might have taken them a while to pluck up the
courage to ask me. I think I told them rather than
them asking me. And they just said 'Don't. If you
ever feel like that, come to us first.' I suppose it's
really them − if I hadn't a family behind me, I
probably wouldn't be talking now.*

Jack, aged 15

Drinking

*I used to drink a lot. It was good a lot of the time
'cos no matter what happened, you didn't care
about it. You didn't have a clue what was going on.*

Martin, aged 15

Drugs

*The only time I could relax was when I was
smoking (hash). That was the only time I felt
OK. ... I was smoking more and more. ... It's
really easy to get into that.*

Brian, aged 16

What they thought had caused them to feel the way they did

Just over one-third of the young people mentioned family
difficulties as one of the main reasons for how they felt.
Parents arguing and fighting, and parental separation
were most commonly mentioned:

*It was about 4 years ago when my parents separated. Since then nothing has really been the same,
kind of. When my parents separated first, I was
young and I wasn't really sure what was going
on. And now, you know, they're fighting still.
They are separated, but they're still fighting now.
They don't talk to each other much, except when*

*they have to, and they are still fighting now. I
suppose I'm kind of getting used to it by now.*

Gary, aged 14

*I wouldn't say I was depressed when it first
happened* [her parents' separation]. *I was sad
and it affected me big time, but I wouldn't say I
was depressed. But after about a year I really
started to notice that there was a big change in
me. I didn't feel right. I was sad all the time. I
found school really difficult. I found it really difficult to talk to people and I lost my confidence.*

Sue, aged 15

*I used to come home from school and they would
still be fighting. I used to sort of hope they were
fighting about me. That was better than them
fighting about my mother's drinking. If it was
about me, maybe they wouldn't split up.*

Brian, aged 16

Bullying was given as a reason by one-fifth of the young
people. This had often gone on for long periods and
involved constant hassle or 'slagging' by 'friends'. They
had usually not told anyone about the bullying until it
came to light through a crisis, such as a suicide attempt:

*In school people would ask for a loan of my stuff
and never give it back. In the yard I'd have to be
on my own, no one would let me do anything. I just
got picked on for everything − like really stupid
stuff. Like kids can be so cruel. ... Em, I'm
really bad at thinking, I've kind of blocked it out.
... There wasn't a lot of violent hitting, but when it
was, it really was. ... Do you know what I mean?*

Then like all those petty comments everyday, they would get to me more than being beaten up.

Paul, aged 13

I was so depressed that I actually became physically sick, so I was brought to hospital and they were going to do a biopsy or something. Then for some reason they got a psychologist up and they found out about the bullying.

Brian, aged 14

Almost one-quarter of the young people interviewed did not identify any particular reason for becoming depressed.

What they thought had helped them to get through their difficult times

Telling someone about what was going on for them was the factor most often reported as being of help to the young people. Three-quarters mentioned this as being helpful. They most often mentioned a parent as the person they told first, usually their mother, or sometimes their father or an older brother or sister. Telling friends was also helpful, but this usually came after they had told parents:

For me, it was talking about it to my mum. Telling someone what went on and they were listening. So I think it was talking to people that helped instead of having to keep it in all the time.

Kate, aged 15

Being able to talk about it was good. I talked to my mum about it. That helped 'cos I got stuff off my chest. She said to me she's not a doctor so she couldn't do things to make me better, but just actually to talk about it helped anyway.

Mark, aged 14

My family were always there – they were fantastic. I could talk to them and they never felt, you know, annoyed with me. Even though school was awful, I always looked forward to going home.

Don, aged 16

Almost three-quarters of the young people mentioned that *doing something to distract themselves* when they felt really bad was very helpful. This was sometimes a very ordinary activity like going for a walk or listening to music. Being able to do *something creative*, such as art, writing lyrics or making something, were activities which helped the young people get through their difficulties:

Music can let you free your emotions.

Gerry, aged 14

Music was a kind of therapy for me. There were different kinds of music I'd listen to if I was feeling good or bad. I'd listen to music that suited the situation.

Mark, aged 14

[Art] helped me to relax really. It allowed me to express myself creatively instead of aggression, like releasing aggression and tearing the place apart. It really just gave me something to do, and something to be proud of.

David, aged 16

I'd go on walks with my friends. I'd try to do something instead of just sitting on the road and doing nothing. It keeps your mind off it, and you get to clear your head.

Vicky, aged 14

Self-reliance was mentioned by a number of young people as being helpful. This included trying to work things out for themselves and making themselves do things that were hard to do:

Like even if you're feeling bad you should push yourself to go to school and stuff. 'Cos no one likes school, but you should 'cos, I dunno, it's weird but you're better off going.

Mark, aged 14

It was just being alone and thinking about it. I think that was the main thing that helped.

Shellie, aged 15

Two young people had found *alternative therapies* helpful (acupuncture and craniosacral therapy):

You'd have to go to it [acupuncture] *to know what it's like. There are pressure points all over the body that relieve tension and stress, and sometimes illness. And you just feel so much better. The day you get it you feel absolutely knackered, but a few days afterwards it's great.*

Ken, aged 14

Fifteen of the 21 participants had attended some form of *professional help*, including counselling or therapy. The vast majority had found this a positive experience and believed it had helped them:

It gives me someone to talk to and more support. And even some ideas that might help. Basically it allows me to talk about my feelings and everything.

Wendy, aged 14

The person I came to see was really good. I could tell her anything, like, just talk about it.

Ciaran, aged 15

I had someone to talk to. Things that would seem really trivial to someone else, they seemed really interested.

Aaron, aged 14

Two of the young people had more mixed views on the professional help they had received:

You'd go there about maybe twice a week or something, and that would just become extra hassle. And all you'd want to do is sit and relax or on Saturday go out with your friends. And the last thing you want to do is get dragged out into town to some hospital, sit for half and hour in some strange place decorated to look like its amiable for kids, but it's really just a big white room with Snow White on the wall or something. You sit there for half an hour, then go in and talk for an hour. And you come out feeling tired, just tired from not doing anything, from having to get up early, bored 'cos you're bored, and with a prescription under your arm for however many pills. And there are points when its helpful, but at the time it's just seen as yet another obstacle, yet another straw on the pile of straws that's turning out to be a bit too much for the camel.

David, aged 16

I mean that in itself is not an enjoyable experience, going and talking to people. It's unpleasant to say those things, you don't really want to. . . . The thing you want to do most is to forget about them and try to move on. . . . But would that have helped? I don't really know.

Bill, aged 15

Two of the young people were very critical of the professional help they received:

I didn't really like the psychologist. It was like I was 7 and they were using baby words and stuff. I know this sounds really arrogant, but I was an intelligent kid and I wasn't going to go along with it.

Eddie, aged 14

The questions they asked were really patronising. The way they'd even look at you, really kind of stern, not relaxed. You felt like you were in a prison cell . . . and you always felt like they thought you were making stuff up.

Jason, aged 15

Nine of the 21 young people had been treated with *anti-depressant medication* and 6 of them had found this very helpful:

I didn't really want to [take medication] at first, 'cos I thought it would be just a bit weird. But then I just sort of said 'I wanna get better so I should definitely'. . . . It's been grand . . . it doesn't work the moment you take it . . . you don't just 'bam' feel

*better, but after a few weeks or so, you do. I felt
sort of more energetic and back to myself.*

Paul, aged 14

*I think the medication I'm on is good. It helps me
feel not worried or something. It helps me not get
angry at as much stuff as I used to. I wouldn't
tell anyone I was on medication, because they'd
probably think, you know, I don't know the word
... mad ... not mad ... but you know what I mean.*

Nessa, aged 14

*I gave them [antidepressant medication] a go and
I think it helped. I'm not sure, it's kind of ridicu-
lous, how can a tablet change the way I think? I'm
not sure − maybe it's just me thinking it's making
me feel better.*

John, aged 15

Two of the young people had more mixed views about
antidepressant medication:

*I haven't really noticed any difference, but my mam
and dad were in here with me the last time I was in,
and they said to the doctor that they had noticed a
big difference in me, that I've been perkier around
the house and doing more stuff.*

Peter, aged 15

*After x many weeks on those pills you seem much
more peppy and alive − well, at least that's
everyone else's observation. I mean, from my own
viewpoint, I find it difficult to be able to step back
and say 'Hey, I'm not feeling sad right now.' Oh, I
dunno. ... I suppose for one thing I don't want to
do that because I want to enjoy the time I have*

right now. It might come back if I think about it for too long.

Frank, aged 16

One young person had very negative views of medication and had refused to take it:

The idea of having to take something to try and help yourself – I hated it. You should be able to help yourself and not depend on medication or whatever to help you.

Sue, aged 15

Conclusion

The results of this study cannot necessarily be applied to *all* young people with depression – other young people may have very different views. These young people volunteered to take part. They may have been more articulate than usual, better able to talk about their experiences and more positive in their views. Despite these possible reservations, what they have to say is very interesting. Telling someone how they were feeling when they were depressed was seen by them as highly important in helping them to get through their 'difficult time', and this someone was most often a parent. Music, art and creative expression helped to carry them through, and using activity as a way of managing the bad times was something they rated highly. Their views on professional input and the use of antidepressant medication, which were so clearly expressed, help us to better understand the struggle experienced by young people in accepting formal 'help' and challenge us as professionals to make our help more relevant and tailored to their needs.

Interactive CD-ROM

We are indebted to these young people for their time, openness and honesty. Some of them are currently involved in making an interactive CD-ROM for other young people with depression, in which they tell their stories and show what helped them, using animation, art, poetry, cartoon and photography. We anticipate that this will help many other young people with depression, showing them that others have felt as they do, that they are not 'mad' and that they will get through it. The CD-ROM will be available in early 2004. Please check www.parentsplus.ie for up-to-date details.

11

Depression – what does the future hold?

Most young people with depressive disorders get better. Research studies consistently show that when teenagers with depressive disorders are followed up, 70–80% of them have improved considerably 2 years after their initial diagnosis. This improvement is not linked to any particular treatment approach and in some cases occurs in children who have not received any formal treatment. This is very encouraging, but much can happen during the course of the depression that can affect the child's future. Relationships may be damaged, educational opportunities may be missed, even lives lost. So, it is well worth seeking help for young people with severe depressive disorders, with a view to bringing about early recovery.

One of the main concerns of most parents of a youngster who has had an episode of depression is that the depression will return. This is particularly so if there is a strong family history of depression, where it may be known that some relatives struggled all their lives with depression.

The statistics

There have been a number of research studies that have followed up young people who have been diagnosed with depressive disorders in adolescence. Results of these studies show that between 40 and 60% of young people who have had a depression disorder in adolescence will have another episode of depression in adult life. This may sound very high, but it is important to realise that it also means that somewhere between 40 and 60% of such young people will never have another episode of depression.

Who is most at risk of having another episode? It is not possible, with our current state of knowledge, to predict the risk for any individual child or teenager. There are some general pointers, but they do not indicate risk for the individual. For instance, we know that those young people who come from families where several members have suffered from depression have a higher risk of recurrence of their depression than those without such a family history. We also know that those who are struggling with ongoing difficulties, such as conflict between their parents, inability to make friends or school failure, are at higher risk. The statistics show us that these are 'risk factors' for relapse, but that does not mean that children living in such circumstances are inevitably going to have further episodes of depression.

Some of these risk factors are out of your control – you cannot change your family history, you cannot make friends for your teenager. But there are things you can do. You can try to foster self-confidence in your child, perhaps by using some of the ideas in Chapter 7. If your child is feeling more confident, he is more likely to make friends. You can try to do something to improve

the situation if there is conflict or very poor communication between you as parents. This is so whether you are
living together or apart.

Having helped your child through depression, you
will be very 'tuned in' to picking up the warning signs
of a further episode of depression. You will know what
helped the last time and will have good ideas about how
best to support your young person to get help early, which
may avoid another full-blown episode of depression. If
your child has had mental health treatment, part of this
will have involved helping the young person to recognise
the 'warning signs' and to have a plan of what to do if he
believes he is relapsing.

'Good effects' of depression?

Are there any 'good effects' of depression? No one would
wish depression on anyone, and it is impossible to see any
'good effects' when your youngster is going through a
depressive disorder. But when they have come out the
other side, it is often possible to see how they have
grown and matured. Getting over depression requires
courage and hard work, and you can be very proud of
your youngster who has achieved this. If you can find a
way of letting him know you feel like this, it may also help
him to see himself in a new light.

Young people who have suffered from depression
often show understanding and compassion to other
people who are going through a difficult time. They
know that things are often not as they seem on the
surface. Having experienced 'the dark and the depths'
themselves, they are often sensitive to other people who
are struggling. In our research with young people who

have recovered from depression (see Chapter 10), we have been very moved by the generosity and enthusiasm of these young people, who have given their ideas and time to develop an interactive CD-ROM for other young people who are going through depression. They have shared their stories and their ideas about what helped them to get better, with a view to helping other young people who are currently experiencing depression.

The brain and depression – current research

There is a great deal of current research into the genetics of depression and into changes in the way the brain functions in depression. This research will hopefully lead us in the near future to have a much better understanding of some of the physical aspects of depression. But we are still a long way from having a clear understanding of why and how depression develops and, perhaps more importantly, why and how recovery happens.

It may be possible in the future for people to have genetic studies carried out, to ascertain whether they have a genetic vulnerability to depression. Would you want to know? I would only want to know if there were steps I could take to avoid getting depression, despite my genetic vulnerability. Maybe there will be a way of changing the genes of people with a genetic vulnerability, or perhaps there will be a special type of anti-depressant medication that will be able to counteract the genetic vulnerability – who knows? Maybe it will be possible to 'train your brain' to think in a certain way, to counteract any genetic vulnerability – to practise a type of 'psychological immunization'?

These ideas may sound slightly 'off the wall', but we cannot predict what the world will be like for our children. Advances in research help to keep hope alive, and hope is in itself a powerful antidote to depression.

Future possibilities are endless, and perhaps the biggest bonus of this type of research will be to reduce the stigma surrounding depression, as we learn to understand better the complexities behind it.

The future and your child

Many parents speak of the joy they feel as their young person gradually emerges from a depressive disorder. Seeing a smile, hearing him laugh or sing, hearing him playing his music again – all such ordinary things in themselves, but sources of delight and wonder to parents of a youngster with depression.

Your support is of vital importance. You cannot make the depression go away, but you can 'walk the road' with your child, keeping a connection and keeping hope alive. It can be a long and difficult road, but you and your child will reach the end of it, stronger and wiser.

Good luck on your journey!

Resources

Resources in your community

- Family and friends.
- Your child's teacher, year head or school counsellor.
- Your family doctor may be able to help directly, or may suggest referral to counselling services or your local Child and Adolescent Mental Health Service (CAMHS).

Books – specifically on helping depressed young people

Published in UK

So Young, So Sad, So Listen by Philip Graham and Carol Hughes (London: Gaskell, 1995). Easy to read, informative, short book for parents about depression in children and teenagers.

Published in USA

A Parents Guide to Childhood and Adolescent Depression by Patricia Gottlieb Shapiro (New York: Dell Publishing, 1994).
Depression Is the Pits, but I'm Getting Better – A Guide for Adolescents by E. Jare Garland (Washington, DC: Magination Press, 1997). Down to earth, easy to read, self-help book for teenagers.

General parenting books

When Parents Separate: A Guide to Helping Your Children Cope by John Sharry, Peter Reid and Eugene Donohoe (Dublin: Veritas, 2001). A straightforward guide for parents that is full of practical information to help children cope with their parents' separation.
Parent Power. Bringing Up Responsible Children and Teenagers by John Sharry (Chichester, UK: Wiley). A parenting guide to managing conflict and getting on better with children and teenagers, expanding on the ideas covered in Chapter 7 of this book.
Taking Charge of ADHD by R. Barkley (New York: Guilford Press, 2000).
Surviving the Leaving Cert: Points for Parents by Marie Murray (Dublin: Veritas, 2002).

Intervention packages

Working Things Out – Young People Overcoming Problems
by Eileen Brosnan, Carol Fitzpatrick, John Sharry,
Jean Forbes and Carla Mills (2004). This is an interactive CD-ROM that contains the stories and experiences of young people who have overcome depression
and other problems (see Chapter 10), which can be used
as an educational tool with young people individually or
in groups.

Parents Plus Families and Adolescents Progamme by John
Sharry and Carol Fitzpatrick (2001). This is a video-
based package that forms the basis of a seven week
group for parents coping with the normal ups or
downs of parenting a teenager as well as those dealing
with specific problems.

For more details on both packages contact Parents Plus,
c/o Mater Child Guidance Clinic, Mater Hospital, North
Circular Road, Dublin 7 (www.parentsplus.ie).

Organisations

Young Minds A UK-based charity committed to
improving the mental health of all children (tel: 044
207 336 8445. Email: enquiries@youngminds.org.uk).
Young Minds runs a Parents' Information Service (tel:
0800 018 2138) that provides information and advice for
anyone with concerns about the mental health of a child
or young person.

Aware An Irish organisation for people with depression
and their families. It provides information, education

and support. Much of its work is with families of young
people with depression:

72, Lower Leeson Street
Dublin 2
Helpline: (01) 676 6166
Website: www.aware.ie

The Manic Depression Fellowship   A UK-based organisation that offers support to people whose lives are
affected by manic depressive disorder (bipolar
disorder):

MDF National Office
CastleWorks
21 St George's Rd
London SE1 6ES
Tel: 0207793 2600
Website: www.mdf.org.uk

Samaritans   A 24-hour service offering confidential
support to anyone who is in crisis:

UK Telephone Helpline: 08457 90 90 90
Irish Telephone Helpline: 1 850 60 90 90

Drugs Advisory and Treatment Centre   Useful source of
information for Irish parents concerned about their
child's drug use. Will be able to advise on local
services and how to access them.

Trinity Court
30–31 Pearse St.
Dublin 2
Tel: 01 677 1122

Websites

www.about-teen-depression.com Useful information with extracts from 'real life' situations. Gives a good overview of therapies.

www.rcpsych.ac.uk Website of the Royal College of Psychiatrists. Click onto Publications, then Factsheets and Leaflets, then Factsheet 25 of the Mental Health and Growing Up series. Good description of depression in children and adolescents, and how to access services.

www.aacap.org Website of the American Academy of Child and Adolescent Psychiatry. Click onto Facts for Families. Gives a good overview of depression in childhood and adolescence.

www.readthesigns.org Excellent interactive site for young people aged 14–25 on a range of mental health problems.

www.youthinmind.net Site to help stressed children and teenagers, and those who care for them. Has excellent guide to services available in the UK.

www.youngminds.org.uk The Young Minds (see above) website. Good advice for parents and carers about what to take seriously, how to help and how to access services.

www.depressioninteenagers.com Visually appealing interactive website based in Edinburgh, with good advice and self-help techniques for teenagers with depression.

www.ru-ok.com Interactive and informative self-help website for teenagers and their parents.

Index